D1556151

50 Shared texts

Photocopiable texts for shared reading

- Fiction, non-fiction, poetry and drama
- Annotated versions
- Discussion prompts

Andrew Taylor

Credits

Author
Andrew Taylor

Assistant Editor
Dulcie Booth

Series Consultants
Fiona Collins and
Alison Kelly

Series Designer
Anna Oliwa

Editor
Roanne Charles

Designers
Anna Oliwa and
Paul Cheshire

Text © 2003 Andrew Taylor
© 2003 Scholastic Ltd

Designed using Adobe InDesign

Published by Scholastic Ltd
Villiers House
Clarendon Avenue
Leamington Spa
Warwickshire CV32 5PR

www.scholastic.co.uk

Printed by Bell and Bain Ltd, Glasgow

7 8 9   7 8 9 0 1 2

British Library Cataloguing-in-Publication Data
A catalogue record for this book is available from the British Library.

ISBN 0-439-98482-3
ISBN 978-0439-98482-9

Contents

N Teacher's notes   P Photocopiable

Term 2

N   **P**

Term 3

N   **P**

N *Teacher's notes*   **P** *Photocopiable*

Introduction

In *50 Shared texts* you will find a range of texts for use in shared reading. In recent years shared text work has become the focal point of daily literacy work, and the success of such shared work is clearly linked to the quality and choice of text. Better understanding of children's reading and writing development has led to the realisation that a greater range of text types, or genres, is needed to enrich children's literacy development. For the busy classroom teacher, seeking out such a range of quality texts can be too time-consuming, which is why appropriate texts have been provided in this book.

Shared reading

Shared reading is at the heart of the activities in this book and is a cornerstone of the National Literacy Strategy, which states that through shared reading children *begin to recognise important characteristics of a variety of written texts, often linked to style and voice.*

First developed in New Zealand by Don Holdaway, shared reading has been a significant literacy routine for children since the 1980s. Holdaway's research and pioneering work in schools brought the benefits of sharing enlarged texts or Big Books to teachers' attention. From his observations of very young children attending to bedtime stories on a one-to-one basis he realised that a similar intimacy with print could be offered through sharing an enlarged text with a group or class of children. He showed how engagement with Big Books can teach children about the characteristics of different text types, their organisation and distinguishing features, as well as the finer details of print. For example, depending on the teacher's focus, an enlarged recipe could be used at text level to model the way a piece of instructional writing is structured, at sentence level to look at the use of imperative verbs or at word level to focus on a particular phoneme. In relation to literature, the meaning of a poem can be explored at text level, the poet's choice

of verbs at sentence level and the rhyming pattern at word level. So, shared reading not only encourages the class to share the actual reading aloud of a text but also enables the teacher to discuss certain language features and support the children in both comprehending and responding to the text.

With younger children, shared reading involves following the text with a pointer to highlight key early concepts of print such as directionality and one-to-one correspondence. With such concepts securely in place, a rather different technique is needed for older children where the focus shifts more to understanding and responding to the text as well as discussing vocabulary and linguistic features. For all children, often the talk surrounding the reading is as important as the reading itself.

Finding the right quality texts for shared reading that will engage and interest the children, as well as meeting the many NLS objectives, can be a difficult task. Once a text is found, you need to identify salient features at word, sentence and text level.

Shared reading is also the springboard for shared writing, guided reading/writing and independent work. Both guided reading and writing provide opportunities for you to guide, support, model and comment on children's response to a text. Activities may involve reading aloud, role-play, performance or writing for a particular purpose. Independent activities may mirror these but need to be clearly structured to enable the children to work independently.

About this book

The texts in this book are organised term by term, following the NLS framework, so there are examples of fiction, poetry, plays and non-fiction.

For each text, both a blank and annotated version are provided. The former is for use with children and can either be enlarged or projected on an overhead projector; the latter is for teacher information and identifies the features of the text and links with NLS objectives.

Background

Background information is provided for each text. This will contextualise the extract, fill in any necessary details and give facts about its author as relevant. Information on themes, technical features or other related texts might also feature here.

Shared reading and discussing the text

This section offers guidance on ways of managing discussion around the text, as well as ways of organising the shared reading. Depending on the age of the children, and demands of the text, different strategies for working with the whole class on the text are given, as well as ways of triggering the children's responses. These include structured discussion suggestions, ideas for role-play, and performance techniques.

Activities

Building on the reading and discussion, this section suggests activities for both whole-class work and guided or independent group work. There are ideas for further textual analysis, sometimes involving shared writing. As in the previous section, talk is pivotal in developing the children's understanding.

Extension/further reading

Suggestions for taking activities into a broader context and ideas for linked reading are also provided, where appropriate. Reading may include books of the same genre, or texts that share the theme or the same author.

The texts

The choice of texts has been driven by the need to ensure that these are quality texts both in content and language. It is hoped that among the selection you will find a mixture of authors and texts, both familiar and new. Whole texts have been provided as far as possible so that children have the satisfaction of reading and appreciating a coherent and complete piece of writing.

Longer texts, such as novels, also need to feature in older children's reading, and sometimes more than one extract from the same carefully chosen novel has been included. Bearing in mind that children should experience as much of the novel as they can, it is recommended that you use the background notes to fill the children in on plot detail, and that you read the story to them or have copies, including a taped version, available for their own reading or listening. Other slots in the curriculum can be used for such reading: private reading, homework, independent group work or story time.

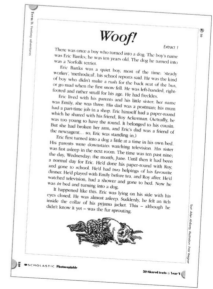

Range and objectives

Year 4 Term 1		
Range	**Text**	**NLS references**
Historical stories	**'The Outlaw Robin Hood'** (extract 1) from *The Outlaw Robin Hood* by Julian Atterton (Walker Books)	S3, T1, T2, T3, T4
	'The Outlaw Robin Hood' (extract 2) from *The Outlaw Robin Hood* by Julian Atterton (Walker Books)	W7, S3, T1, T2, T3, T9, T11, T12, T15
	'The Lady of Fire and Tears' (extract 1) from *The Lady of Fire and Tears* by Terry Deary (Orion Children's Books)	W7, W11, S2, T1, T2, T3, T8
	'The Lady of Fire and Tears' (extract 2) from *The Lady of Fire and Tears* by Terry Deary (Orion Children's Books)	T1, T2, T3, T4
Historical stories; recounts	**'The Terrible Tudors'** from *The Terrible Tudors* by Terry Deary (Scholastic Children's Books)	W1, T7, T8, T17
Poems based on common themes	**'Mary Celeste'** from *Midnight Forest* by Judith Nicholls (Faber & Faber)	T1, T7, T14
	'Legend' from *The North Ship* by Philip Larkin (Faber & Faber)	T1, T7, T14
	'Wind' from *Earth Magic* by Dionne Brand (Sister Vision Press)	S3, T14
Playscripts	**'Charlie and the Chocolate Factory: A Play'** (extract 1) from *Charlie and the Chocolate Factory: A Play* by Roald Dahl and Richard R George (Puffin Books)	T1, T5, T6, T13
	'Charlie and the Chocolate Factory: A Play' (extract 2) from *Charlie and the Chocolate Factory: A Play* by Roald Dahl and Richard R George (Puffin Books)	S4, T4, T5, T6, T13
Newspaper articles	**'Hero worship'** from *Sunday Times* (News International)	T16, T18, T19, T20
Newspaper reports	**'They all kept on running'** from *Whitby Gazette* (Yorkshire Regional Newspapers)	T18, T19, T20, T24
News reports	**'Seven feared dead in space shuttle disaster'** from *Guardian Unlimited* website	T20, T21, T24
Instructions	**'Riding on difficult surfaces'** from *Mountain Bikes* by Janet Cook (Usborne)	T22, T25, T26
	'Mud, snow, sand and ice' from *Mountain Bikes* by Janet Cook (Usborne)	S1, T22, T25, T26
Reports: encyclopedia entry	**'Robin Hood'** from *Oxford Children's Encyclopedia* (Oxford University Press)	T17, T26, T27
	'Anansi' from *Oxford Children's Encyclopedia* (Oxford University Press)	T17, T27

Year 4 Term 2

Range	Text	NLS references
Science fiction	**'A Hole in the Head'** (extract 1) from *A Hole in the Head* by Nicholas Fisk (Walker Books)	S2, T1, T2, T4
	'A Hole in the Head' (extract 2) from *A Hole in the Head* by Nicholas Fisk (Walker Books)	S2, T1, T2, T4, T10
Fantasy adventures	**'Beyond the Deepwoods'** from *Beyond the Deepwoods* by Paul Stewart (Corgi Children's Books)	W9, S1, T1, T4, T10
	'Woof!' (extract 1) from *Woof!* by Allan Ahlberg (Viking Kestrel)	T1, T2, T13
	'Woof!' (extract 2) from *Woof!* by Allan Ahlberg (Viking Kestrel)	S1, T2, T4, T5, T13
	'Storm' (extract 1) from *Storm* by Kevin Crossley-Holland (Mammoth)	W1, S1, T1, T2, T4
	'Storm' (extract 2) from *Storm* by Kevin Crossley-Holland (Mammoth)	W9, S1, T2, T4, T13
Poems from different cultures	**'Granny Granny Please Comb My Hair'** by Grace Nichols from *Can I Buy a Slice of Sky?* edited by Grace Nichols (Hodder)	W1, T4, T5, T7, T11
	'The Older the Violin the Sweeter the Tune' by John Agard from *Say It Again, Granny* edited by Grace Nichols (Bodley Head)	W1, T4, T5, T7, T11
	'Honey I Love' by Eloise Greenfield from *Can I Buy a Slice of Sky?* edited by Grace Nichols (Hodder)	W9, S4, T4, T7, T11
Classic poetry	**'Windy Nights'** from *A Child's Garden of Verses* by Robert Louis Stevenson (Puffin Books)	S4, T4, T7, T11
	'The Listeners' from *The Complete Works* by Walter de la Mare (Faber & Faber)	W11, T4, T5, T6, T7
	'The Way Through the Woods' from *Selected Poetry* by Rudyard Kipling (Penguin Books)	T4, T6, T7
Information texts on similar themes	**'Rivers'** from *Oxford Children's Encyclopedia* (Oxford University Press)	W3, T17, T18, T21
	'Fact File' from *Rivers* by Richard Stephens (Eagle Books)	T17, T18, T21, T23
Explanation texts	**'Brains'** from *Oxford Children's Encyclopedia* (Oxford University Press)	W1, W3, S4, T18, T19, T20
	'Bulging brain basics' from *Bulging Brains* by Nick Arnold (Scholastic Children's Books	T9, T18, T19, T20, T25

Year 4 Term 3

Range	Text	NLS references
Stories that raise issues	**'Bella's Den'** (extract 1) from *Bella's Den* by Berlie Doherty (Mammoth)	T1, T3, T11
	'Bella's Den' (extract 2) from *Bella's Den* by Berlie Doherty (Mammoth)	T1, T3, T11, T12
	'The Angel of Nitshill Road' (extract 1) from *The Angel of Nitshill Road* by Anne Fine (Egmont)	S2, T1, T11
	'The Angel of Nitshill Road' (extract 2) from *The Angel of Nitshill Road* by Anne Fine (Egmont)	T1, T3, T8, T11, T20, T24
Stories that raise issues; stories from other cultures	**'Journey to Jo'burg'** (extract 1) from *Journey to Jo'burg* by Beverley Naidoo (Armada)	S4, T1, T2, T3, T8
	'Journey to Jo'burg' (extract 2) from *Journey to Jo'burg* by Beverley Naidoo (Armada)	T1, T2, T3, T8
	'Lord of the Winds' from *Lord of the Winds* by Maggie Pearson (Magi Publications)	T1, T2, T15
Poetry in different forms	**'The Magic Box'** by Kit Wright from *Can I Buy a Slice of Sky?* edited by Grace Nichols (Hodder)	T4, T6, T7, T9, T14
	'Moon haiku'	T5, T6, T7, T14, T15
	'Timothy Winters' from *Going to the Fair* by Charles Causley (Viking Kestrel)	T4, T6, T7, T9
	'Early in the morning' and **'There once was a man'** from *Selected Poems for Children* by Charles Causley (Macmillan Children's Books)	T4, T6, T7, T9, T14
Discussion texts	**'Animal Rights and Wrongs'** from *Animal Rights and Wrongs* by Lesley Newson (A&C Black)	T16, T17, T20, T21
Persuasive writing	**'Why kill whales?'** from *Saving the Whale* by Michael Bright (Aladdin Books)	S4, T16, T18, T20, T21, T24
	'The Song of the Whale' from *Hot Dog and Other Poems* by Kit Wright (Viking Kestrel)	T4, T6, T9, T17, T18
	'Jorvik' from the 2003 Jorvik leaflet (Jorvik Centre)	W15, T18, T19, T25
	'Charity appeals' press advertisements (Oxfam and Concern)	S4, T17, T18, T19, T25

The Outlaw Robin Hood

by Julian Atterton

Extract 1

Background

This extract is taken from *Robin Hood and Little John*, one of two books in *The Outlaw Robin Hood*. The original stories are very old (see the encyclopedia entry on page 40.) Although not strictly a historical story, the piece is clearly set within a particular historical context.

The extract opens with Robin walking off angrily into the forest after an argument with his outlaws. He meets a 'giant' who later becomes known as Little John.

Shared reading and discussing the text

● Read the extract and clarify any unfamiliar language. Model how the context can help in understanding vocabulary. Use a dictionary to check the meaning suggested by the context.

● Before re-reading, ask the children to focus carefully on Robin, the time of day and the setting. Read the first two paragraphs. Ask the children to discuss in pairs their ideas about the setting and character before sharing them. Reinforce understanding of how the writer sets the scene for the action that follows.

● Ask half the class to focus on Robin, the other half on the giant, particularly on the way each speaks. Read on and then let them discuss their ideas before you collect them in a table.

● Look closely at the giant, marking his speech and the descriptions of him. Notice how the descriptions reflect his character. Can the children see anything strange, and humorous, in the way the giant behaves after he has pushed Robin in the stream? How would they explain what he says at the end? (He seems to be sorry and surprised at what he has done, whereas a moment ago he was rude and aggressive.)

● Point out that while several hours pass in the first paragraph, the main part of the extract describes an event that only takes a few minutes. Can the children say why this is? (The author has selected events to highlight, providing just enough information to set the scene and create atmosphere before giving interesting or exciting events in more detail,

building up tension and creating conflict.)

● Model how writers use this technique by rewriting the extract together. Use a few sentences to set the context, speaking about the choices you are making and why. For example: *Robin slept for a few hours. After a few hours, he woke and started to make his way home. He came to a bridge across a stream.* In your next sentences, explain that you want to slow the action down to concentrate on the important event – the fight between Robin and the giant. Ask children to contribute effective words and sentences to the draft.

Activities

● Use the text as a cloze procedure, removing some of the verbs. Children should work in pairs to discuss alternatives and consider which verb is most powerful in the context. Use a plenary session to evaluate the children's choices. Select the verbs carefully to make the task appropriate for different levels of ability.

● Ask children to re-read the text to make a labelled map of the setting, marking in the physical features and indicating where particular events occurred.

● Make a table for the group to collect together at least three bullet points about both Robin and the giant that can be justified by giving examples from the text.

● Ask less confident writers, working as a group, to retell the story. Remind them of the shared writing work and agree content. Recap how the opening paragraph should set the scene, then the action should slow to give more detail about the fight. Stop them frequently to reflect on the writing as it progresses.

Extension/further reading

Explain that Robin Hood was an outlaw because he disapproved of the way the land was unfairly ruled by the rich. Debate whether breaking the law can ever be justified.

There are many retellings of Robin Hood's adventures. A favourite is *The Story of Robin Hood* retold by Robert Leeson (Kingfisher).

4: 1: T1: to investigate how settings and characters are built up from small details, and how the reader responds to them

4: 1: T2: to identify the main characteristics of the key characters, drawing on the text to justify views, and using the information to predict actions

4: 1: T3: to explore chronology in narrative by mapping how much time passes in the course of the story, e.g. noticing where there are jumps in time, or where some events are skimmed over quickly, and others told in detail

Extract 1

The Outlaw Robin Hood

Robin walked until his anger was cooled by the peace of the forest. Some hours later he was dozing against a tree when the distant sound of vesper bells told him it was time to turn back towards the clearing where the outlaws had their camp.

On his way homewards he came to a swift flowing stream over which a trunk had been laid to serve as a bridge. As Robin stepped onto it, a giant of a man appeared out of the trees on the other bank, and without so much as a glance at Robin he stepped up onto the far end of the trunk.

"Not so fast, good fellow," cried Robin. "I was here before you, and I claim the right to cross first."

"Get out of my way, you dung-beetle," growled the giant, and he lumbered towards Robin so that they met in the middle of the bridge. Robin looked up at his opponent and shivered, for the giant wore a hood, and all that could be seen of his face in the evening shadows was a tangle of beard and a crooked row of teeth.

"It seems like you need a lesson in courtesy," said Robin, and he thumped the giant in the chest. But the giant stood as solid as a rock, and before Robin could strike again he reached out with a huge hand and gave Robin a shove that sent him flying off the bridge into the stream.

Soaked and spluttering, Robin crawled up through the brambles and nettles of the river-bank to find the giant squatting on the ground, with his hands covering his face.

"That was not like me," said the giant. "Not like me at all."

implies something had made him angry before this extract begins

1st paragraph establishes time and place – the setting; several hours pass in paragraph 1

more detail about setting, helps to create drama

evident contrast in the way the two speak

suggests secretive, mysterious

Robin is more polite than John

alliteration

in paragraphs 2–7, only a few minutes pass

associates Robin with nature

evening church service

those who live outside the law

from Robin's point of view the giant is frightening and monstrous – revealed through a few effective details

suggests that the giant was not trying to hit Robin, perhaps just getting him out of the way

contrast, surprise – strange thing for a man who seemed to want to fight to say, seems to be sorry; author builds up fear and mystery around giant, then surprises reader

4: 1: T4: to explore narrative order: identify and map out the main stages of the story: introductions – build-ups – climaxes or conflicts – resolutions

4: 1: S3: to identify the use of powerful verbs through cloze procedure

The Outlaw Robin Hood
by Julian Atterton

Extract 2

Background

This extract continues the story of Robin Hood's meeting with the giant who became his friend Little John.

Shared reading and discussing the text

● Recap on the previous extract and then read this one. Point out that the sinister, frightening giant has changed. Ask the children to suggest in what ways he is different.

● Focus on the dialogue and how it helps to develop the characters and give background. Highlight some of the interesting synonyms for *said*, for example *exclaimed, replied*. Discuss how a writer varies words and uses powerful language to keep the reader interested.

● Investigate the beginning of this scene by asking children to make a freeze-frame of Robin talking to the giant. Ask how Robin will be feeling at this point. Angry, upset? How could his feelings be expressed in the way he stands? Ask children to check the text for ideas about how Robin and the giant should look.

● After the children have created the physical scene, ask them what the characters might be thinking, For example, Robin might be remembering the fight at Pontefract, the giant remembering the home he has lost. Introduce 'thought-tracking', where the children suggest thoughts running through the minds of the character, speaking in the first person.

● Ask the children to reflect on the freeze-frame and thought-tracking activities. Encourage exploratory discussion by asking questions: *Is there anything in the text that explains why the characters act as they do? Is there anything that suggests Robin would be thinking the way we suggested?*

● Talk about how this extract ends. What is the author setting up to happen next? Presumably Little John will tell the story of how he lost his hearth (home). Ask the children to predict this story, making use of the hints given in this extract and the previous one – something extreme has happened to make Little John act out of character.

Activities

● List ideas about what could have happened to John. (He might have upset the Sheriff of Nottingham, so was driven off his land.) Choose one idea to work on together. Explain that to write the next part of the story, you need a short bridging paragraph to get the characters to a new setting. Model this, then write John's story as he would tell it, in one or two paragraphs. Emphasise that to be interesting the story needs to give details and be written powerfully. Think about the use of strong verbs, for example alternatives for *said*, *went* and *came*. As you write, discuss the tense and point out how you maintain it. Occasionally make some weak verb choices and encourage the children to improve your text.

● Ask children to extend their table of points about the two characters. What more have they learned in this extract?

● Compare the character of Robin Hood in this extract with the previous one. Draw an image of a balance and re-read both texts. Ask the group to collect examples of Robin as aggressive outlaw on one side of the balance and examples of him being kinder on the other. See if they can decide where the change comes and why. For example, is it because he knows he cannot fight this giant, or because he recognises him? An easier option would be to do the same exercise focusing on Little John.

● Ask the group to retell the story in cartoon strip format, identifying the key moments in the narrative. They might add speech bubbles and a short caption to each frame.

Extension and further reading

Collect books, films and illustrations from different retellings of the Robin Hood story, for example Disney's animated version or *Robin Hood Prince of Thieves*. Identify a scene common to a film and these texts, and ask how the film version compares with the text.

Rosemary Sutcliff's *The Chronicles of Robin Hood* (OUP) is a traditional retelling suitable for more confident readers.

4: 1: T1: to investigate how settings and characters are built up from small details, and how the reader responds to them

4: 1: T2: to identify the main characteristics of the key characters, drawing on the text to justify views, and using the information to predict actions

4: 1: T3: to explore chronology in narrative, noticing where there are jumps in time, or where some events are skimmed over quickly, and others told in detail

Extract 2

The Outlaw Robin Hood

Shaking his head sadly, he looked up at Robin, and after one good look at the giant's face, Robin gave a gasp of recognition.

"I know you," he exclaimed. "You came to my rescue in the market-place of Pontefract when I was fighting for my life against Guy of Gisburn and his men-at-arms."

"Aye, that was me," replied the giant. "I am glad to see you got away alive."

"And ever since I have been wishing we could meet again so I might thank you," said Robin. "Tell me your name."

"John of Melton," said the giant, but he spoke almost as if he were ashamed of the sound of it.

"And I am Robin Hood," said Robin, holding out his hand.

This time it was the giant who gasped. He eyed Robin from head to toe and gave a grim chuckle.

"Robin Hood," he repeated slowly. "That is a name I hear spoken with fear and trembling from Nottingham to Sherburn. And to think I nearly drowned you! I beg your pardon, great outlaw."

"And I will grant it, Little John," said Robin, "but only if tonight you eat supper with myself and my companions."

"Gladly," answered Little John, "for I no longer have a hearth of my own to go to."

"It sounds to me as if there is a tale in that," said Robin. "Perhaps you will tell it as we eat!"

expresses Robin's surprise

synonyms of 'said' add variation and accuracy

the giant seems changed in this extract – weighed down by sadness

setting up the next part of the story

a wry laugh – John is not happy

John has real respect for Robin

Robin is making a cheeky joke – 'Little' is ironic, because he is anything but little! (this is the first time we hear the famous name)

clearly John has a story to tell

4: 1: T9: to use different ways of planning stories

4: 1: T11: to write character sketches, focusing on small details to evoke sympathy or dislike

4: 1: T12: to write independently, linking own experience to situations in historical stories, e.g. *How would I have responded? What would I do next?*

4: 1: T15: to use paragraphs in story writing to organise and sequence the narrative

4: 1: W7: to spell regular verb endings

4: 1: S3: to identify the use of powerful verbs

The Lady of Fire and Tears by Terry Deary

Extract 1

Background

Terry Deary is best known for his *Horrible Histories*, but he also writes historical novels. The political background to Mary Queen of Scots' execution, to which this extract eludes, is complicated, so you might want to link it to work on the Tudors. Here, Lady Marsden begins to tell the story of Mary's death to her son Will and her servant Meg. Will knows the story, but Meg has not heard it before.

Shared reading and discussing the text

● If you have been working on the Tudors, briefly recap the historical background.

● Prepare to read the text in two sections – the opening paragraph and the rest of the text – pausing between them. Before reading, tell the children there is a clue in the opening paragraph that suggests the storyteller doesn't like telling the story. Identify the phrase with them (*the hurt in her face*). Ask them to talk about why anyone could be hurt by a story.

● Together, identify the verbs in the first paragraph. Ask the children what tense they are written in and how they know. For example, remind them that *-ed* endings indicate the regular past tense.

● Now read the rest of the extract. Clarify the meaning of vocabulary such as *bitter, bleak* and *warrant*. Use a variety of approaches: the sense of the sentence, or looking up words in the dictionary. Where a dictionary definition is found, check that it makes sense in context.

● Remind the children of the discussion about why Lady Marsden found this story so painful. Ask them whether, having read the rest of the extract, any of the explanations now seem more plausible or sensible than others.

● Reinforce the children's understanding that Lady Marsden is telling of an event which happened in her own past. Explain that it is like someone in their family telling a story of what happened a few years ago. You might want to introduce the notion of a story within a story.

● Look at Lady Marsden's storytelling technique by highlighting the paragraphs where she talks of Mary's execution. Help the children to see how the scene is set quickly in terms of time, place, background and atmosphere, before moving to the evening Mary heard the news of her execution. Ask the children if they think Lady Marsden tells the story well and why. (For example, she brings in small details about the weather, the prison and Mary's health which make the event seem real and 'alive'. She also selects details to build up interest and drama.)

Activities

● Focus on the second paragraph. Identify how Lady Marsden places her story very precisely into a specific time. Ask the group why this time setting is important. Ask them to create a timeline by filling in relevant dates, for example 1587 and 1588. Ask them to re-read the paragraph and write a label for the timeline for 1588.

● Ask an able group to use different information sources, including the extract from *The Terrible Tudors* on page 18, to research Mary Queen of Scots and her relationship with Queen Elizabeth. Ask them to report back on whether they think Terry Deary's story is accurate to the known historical facts.

● Ask children to work in pairs to underline where Lady Marsden is sympathetic to Mary and, in another colour, where she is critical about Elizabeth, for example *always threatening to execute her and never having the courage*. Ask them where Lady Marsden's sympathies lay. How do they know?

● A group could re-read and then practise telling the story of Mary's life at Fortheringhay.

Extension and further reading

Use information books to add other significant dates to the timeline. These could relate to Mary or the reign of Elizabeth more generally.

My Friend Walter by Michael Morpurgo (Mammoth) uses the ghost of Sir Walter Raleigh in a modern setting. *The Terrible Tudors* is one of Terry Deary's *Horrible Histories* (Scholastic) and provides an interesting contrast in style.

4: 1: T1: to investigate how settings and characters are built up from small details, and how the reader responds to them

4: 1: T2: to identify the main characteristics of the key characters, drawing on the text to justify views

4: 1: T3: to explore chronology in narrative by mapping how much time passes in the course of the story, e.g. noticing where there are jumps in time, or where some events are skimmed over quickly, and others told in detail

Extract 1

The Lady of Fire and Tears

verbs in the past tense

these memories are painful to Lady Marsden

Mother folded her embroidery, placed it in her lap, and folded her hands over it. I lowered my eyes because I couldn't bear to see the hurt in her face. But Meg turned her great sea-green eyes up to look at my mother, pushed her tangled mane of chestnut hair back from her forehead and rested her pointed chin on one hand.

story within a story, Lady Marsden is remembering something from long before

"I was there when they executed Mary Queen of Scots," my mother began. "It was just before I married your father, Will, and before you were born, of course. It was at this time of the year, February. Fifteen eighty-seven, the year before the Great Armada tried to conquer us. I was with Queen Mary in her room when the Earl of Shrewsbury came to her that night – a bitter, mid-winter night like tonight – and told her she would die at dawn, at eight o'clock."

places the story in a specific time

"Where was this?" Meg asked.

"Fotheringhay Castle in Northamptonshire, two hundred miles south of here. A blcak enough place at the best of times, but when you're a prisoner waiting for your execution it is a cold Hell."

powerful description of the atmosphere in the setting

"So she knew she was going to die," Meg said.

these paragraphs almost delay the story of the execution

"Queen Elizabeth had imprisoned her for eighteen years, always threatening to execute her and never having the courage to sign the order. Queen Mary thought she would die a natural death in her prison. She'd already retired to bed that February night. She suffered terribly from rheumatism and needed all my help to rise and get dressed to meet the earl. When he came into her apartment he had the warrant with the yellow wax seal of England on it."

Lady Marsden seems to sympathise with Mary

"I couldn't stand that," Meg whispered. "Knowing that you're going to be executed in a few hours' time. It's horrible."

"Queen Mary took the news calmly enough," said my mother. "She asked for a Catholic priest so she could say her final prayers. They refused to allow it, of course."

I shook my head. "It couldn't have done any harm. Not then."

4: 1: T8: to find out more about popular authors and use this information to move on to more books by favourite writers

4: 1: S2: to investigate verb tenses

4: 1: W7: to spell regular verb endings

4: 1: W11: to define familiar vocabulary in their own words, using alternative phrases or expressions

The Lady of Fire and Tears by Terry Deary

Extract 2

Background

This extract continues the story of the execution. Lady Marsden is telling Meg about events at Fortheringhay Castle. This passage includes an eyewitness account of the same events.

Shared reading and discussing the text

● Ask the children to summarise important details from the previous extract, for example that, after many years of imprisonment, Mary had been sentenced to death. You might want to use the timeline as an aide-memoire.

● Cover the text except for the first paragraph. Read this to the children. Ask them to discuss in pairs why the author includes so many details. Can they come up with two possible reasons? (For example, they keep you interested, they help a reader to picture the scene.) Share ideas and encourage children to read out any interesting details.

● Point out the sentence *At eight she asked me to go with her to the hall.* What can the children infer from this? (Mary felt in need of support, she must have considered Lady Marsden a special friend.)

● Now read the rest of the extract. Focus on Meg's role and ask the children to underline what Meg says and does. Notice how Meg helps Lady Marsden to tell her story by prompting her for details. Explain that this also has the function of generating extra information for the reader by having a character ask the sorts of questions the reader wants answered.

● Model how to use detail and questions in writing. Agree the details of the story and who is going to tell it, for example the executioner, and another, invented, character, perhaps his assistant. (The assistant effectively replaces Meg in this version.) Explain that you will start by setting out what is going to happen: *Today I was going to cut off Queen Mary's head.* Have one paragraph where the executioner describes getting dressed carefully, a second where he describes his preparations, such as sharpening his axe. Begin each new paragraph with a question from the apprentice to trigger the account the executioner gives. As you write each sentence, explain what you are doing and why. End the piece dramatically, echoing the opening lines: *Everything was ready: my gloves, the cloth, the axe. 'Are you ready boy?' I called. We walked to the door and into the great hall. I was going to cut off Queen Mary's head.*

Activities

● After a careful re-reading of the text, a group could make a labelled plan of the Great Hall, identifying where the main characters are standing. For less confident readers, provide an outline plan with some features marked in or support the activity by using it as the 'response to the text' element of guided reading.

● Ask the group to re-read the text and identify five ways in which Lady Marsden's story makes you feel sympathy for Mary. (For example, she prays, she needs company, she looked like *a bride going to be married to death*, she shows concern for her dog, people have come to watch her die, she is preached at.)

● Children could re-read both extracts and report back on why they would like to read the rest of the novel, or not.

● Follow up the shared reading and writing by helping the children to invent two characters present at Queen Mary's execution, to tell part of the story of the day. Emphasise the use of small details to set the scene, build atmosphere and slow down the action. Suggest they use questions, perhaps from a younger character who does not know what is going on, to trigger the explanation given by the main character.

Extension and further reading

Ask children to use the extracts to compose a letter to Queen Elizabeth telling her about the execution of her cousin, Mary Queen of Scots. The work will be more effective if you model writing a letter in an appropriate formal tone.

Using a variety of historical sources, ask more able children to check how accurate is this retelling of the death of Mary Queen of Scots.

4: 1: T1: to investigate how settings and characters are built up from small details, and how the reader responds to them

4: 1: T2: to identify the main characteristics of the key characters, drawing on the text to justify views, and using the information to predict actions

Extract 2

The Lady of Fire and Tears

"The Queen lay back on the bed and closed her eyes. She couldn't sleep, of course. Not with the marching of the guards outside her door, and the hammering of the carpenters in the great hall. She must have known they were finishing the scaffold that she'd be executed on. She rose at six o'clock and said her prayers alone. At eight she asked me to go with her to the hall. What could I say? I didn't want to see her die, but I couldn't refuse, could I?"

My mother was trembling. Meg touched her hand gently. "No, you couldn't," she murmured.

"We dressed her in her black satin dress. The buttons were black jet trimmed with pearls and made in the shape of acorns. Lovely things. And the sleeves of the dress were slashed to show the purple lining underneath. She had a white veil flowing down her back like a bride. She was a bride going to be married to death."

"Was she afraid?" Meg asked.

"She didn't seem to be. She looked so calm. She petted her little dog and walked down those cold corridors to the great hall."

"They'd have had to carry me," Meg said.

"I didn't know there would be so many people there," my mother said. "Three hundred people crowded into the great hall. The death of a queen is a moment of history. So many people, so quiet. And staring at her. Watching every last movement. Listening to that foolish man, the Dean of Peterborough."

"What did he do?"

"He preached at her and told her to give up her Catholic religion. On and on he went. She simply answered, 'I've lived a Catholic, so I will die a Catholic.'"

"That's what I'd have told him," Meg said fiercely.

---

lots of detail in 1st paragraph 'delays' finding out about the execution

Meg asks questions and comments throughout, breaking up the narrative and keeping it interesting; asks questions reader would want answering

Mary sees Lady Marsden as a friend, someone she wants there at her execution; perhaps Mary is afraid

very precise details help reader imagine the scene

very strong, melodramatic image that makes us sympathise with Mary

makes the Queen seem very human and ordinary – increases sympathy

reminds us that this execution is an important event

4: 1: T3: to explore chronology in narrative by mapping how much time passes in the course of the story, e.g. noticing where there are jumps in time, or where some events are skimmed over quickly, and others told in detail

4: 1: T4: to explore narrative order: identify and map out the main stages of the story: introductions – build-ups – climaxes or conflicts – resolutions

The Terrible Tudors by Terry Deary and Neil Tonge

Background

This extract relates closely to the extracts from *The Lady of Fire and Tears*, describing the part that Elizabeth played in Mary's death, and using an eyewitness account.

The *Horrible Histories* books present information in a conversational, amusing way. Illustrations are cleverly used to add humour. The books are based on thorough knowledge and often make use of incidental details that illuminate the historical period for children.

Shared reading and discussing the text

It might be helpful to display and refer to the extracts from *The Lady of Fire and Tears* throughout the shared work.

● Because of the formality of some of the language, some children might find this extract difficult. Prepare them for the shared text work by reading the text in a guided reading session. As part of the introduction to the text, highlight challenging vocabulary, and any complex sentence structures.

● Read the extract through. Make links with previous reading, and contrast its function and style with *The Lady of Fire and Tears*.

● Identify the use of italic and the lead-in clauses (*This eyewitness described it… Elizabeth did apologise…*) and discuss why italic is used. (To distinguish between the author's words and a direct quotation from an eyewitness.)

● Re-read the paragraph beginning *Kneeling down*. Can the children identify anything from the language used that makes it sound like it was written over 500 years ago? If necessary, prompt them by pointing out the formality of the language, for example *without any fear of death… laid down her head*. Ask them to think how we might report such an execution today.

● Compare the 'narration' of this text with the extracts from *The Lady of Fire and Tears*. Help the children to recognise that in *The Lady of Fire and Tears* Terry Deary is writing as Will and Lady Marsden. Here, although he and Neil Tonge use the words of eyewitnesses, they are also using their own voice. Help the children to

see that in *The Terrible Tudors* the authors comment on events, and in much more informal language: *But that's another story…*

● Ask the children whether they think the author is sympathetic to Elizabeth and believes her 'apology'. Can they find lines in the text that support their views, such as *So that was all right!* where the authors are being ironic?

Activities

● Ask children to compare this extract with Terry Deary's retelling of Mary's execution in *The Lady of Fire and Tears*. What similarities and differences can they find? Use this as the basis of a later guided reading session where you focus on some of the differences between fiction and non-fiction texts.

● Ask the group to consider Terry Deary as a writer. Can they identify five things they like about his writing, drawing from the extracts they have read here and their independent reading? Encourage children to reflect on and discuss their reading and to read other titles written by Terry Deary.

● To reinforce the differences highlighted in this text between Elizabethan language and language today, ask children to work in pairs to create a television or radio commentary on the execution of Mary, using the details given in the different accounts. Give some children the opportunity to perform their commentaries.

Extension and further reading

Ask the children to find another information text about Mary Queen of Scots to compare with this extract. Give them a set of prompts to guide their investigation, for example *Which book gives the most information? Which is easiest to read and why? How could you check whether the texts are accurate or not?*

Ask children to use all the extracts they have read about Mary to prepare a quiz about her in the next history lesson.

Book 3 of John Guy's *Kings and Queens* series (Ticktock Media) presents information in a lively way and makes an interesting comparison.

4: 1: T7: to compare and contrast texts on similar themes, particularly their form and language, discussing personal responses and preferences

4: 1: T8: to find out more about popular authors and use this information to move onto more books by favourite writers

The Terrible Tudors

authorisation

The Queen's mind was greatly troubled. She signed a death warrant for Mary and gave it to Davison, her secretary. The next day she changed her mind but it was too late. The warrant was delivered and Mary was executed. William Davison was fined heavily and put in the Tower of London.

the messenger got the blame

italic used to distinguish types of text

According to one account, Mary was beheaded by a clumsy executioner who took at least three blows of the axe and a bit of sawing to finish the job. This eyewitness described it…

explains why the next 2 paragraphs are important – they are the words of someone who was there at the execution

sounds almost flippant; meant to be humorous; certainly contrasts with the language of the 'eyewitness' account

The executioners desired her to forgive them for her death. She answered, "I forgive you with all my heart for now, I hope, you shall make an end to all my troubles."

Kneeling down upon a cushion, without any fear of death, she spoke a psalm. Then she laid down her head, putting her chin on the block. Lying very still on the block she suffered two strokes with the axe, making very little noise or none at all. And so the executioner cut off her head, sawing one little gristle. He then lifted up her head to the view of all the assembly and cried, "God save the Queen!"

formality of language indicates this was written long ago

author is being ironic – clearly he thinks this 'apology' and denial of blame was not all right

Elizabeth did apologise to Mary's son, James…

My dearest brother, I want you to know the huge grief I feel for something I did not want to happen and that I am innocent in the matter.

So that was all right!

important details that identify historical consequences of the execution

But the Spanish didn't believe in Elizabeth's innocence – they didn't want to. King Philip II of Spain was sick of English ships raiding his own, laden with treasure from his overseas territories. Philip was a Catholic, like Mary. So he used her execution as an excuse to send a huge invasion fleet, the Armada, to take revenge for these English crimes. But that's another story…

4: 1: W1: to read and spell words through using phonic/spelling knowledge as a cue, together with graphic, grammatical and contextual knowledge, when reading unfamiliar texts

4: 1: T17: to identify features of non-fiction texts in print

Mary Celeste

by Judith Nicholls

Background

The *Mary Celeste* was a real ship discovered floating with no one on board, no sign of struggle and no message about where everyone had gone. This poem was written long after the events were supposed to have taken place.

Shared reading and discussing the text

● Read the poem through without initial discussion or explanation. Use your tone of voice to bring out a contrast between the lines in italic and the rest of the poem.

● Ask the children for immediate impressions. What do they think the poem is about? Briefly explain the legend. Explain that you will re-read the poem and want them to notice which verses describe life before everyone went missing and which describe the empty ship.

● Draw out the significance of the first verse. (It describes the empty, mysterious boat.) Is there any hint of what happened, such as evidence of violence, could all the crew have been kidnapped? Ensure the children understand that, in fact, everything seems normal. Notice the gentle rhythm of the opening, reinforced by the rhyme and vocabulary. Point out the line *the hull creaks…* – an ordinary, peaceful scene.

● Ask the children to discuss in pairs why the poet might start the poem like this. (There is no right answer, but by starting from the end and going back to tell the story she emphasises the ordinariness, increases the mystery, and gives the following verses added pathos because we read them in the light of what has happened.)

● Split the children into four groups and give them each a character from the poem. Explain that you will read the poem again and each group should listen and read carefully to find out all they can about their character. Ask inferential questions such as *Do you think the first mate was happy? Why?*

● Help the children to see that the main part of the poem is written in verses of different length, without an obvious rhyme scheme. Each verse is like a separate snapshot. You could use them to build a picture of life on the

ship, by asking children to take on the roles of the people mentioned and act out the verses in mime. Finally, they could hold a freeze-frame position that sums up their character.

● Now highlight the second italicised verse. Can the children identify the three sinister events suggested? Clarify their understanding of the significance of the gulls *wheeling like vultures* (vultures hover above dying creatures), and interpretations of *snatched* (to wake up suddenly, to be taken away by force). Make the point that the poet doesn't tell the reader what has happened, only asks questions.

● Contrast the final verse with the first verse. Can the children identify how the atmosphere has changed? For example, the lullaby is replaced by sighs. Explain the significance of the siren song and the powerful image of the waves echoing on and on.

Activities

● Research the story of the *Mary Celeste*. How does Judith Nicholls' version compare with the information found? In guided reading, discuss the differences between a non-fiction report or explanation and a poem.

● Ask the group to discuss what might have happened to the people on board. Children could write their ideas onto paper shaped like a ship's wheel or sail and create a display.

● Write a series of statements about the poem in one column of a four-column table. Head the other three columns *Yes*, *No*, and *No evidence*. The statements should present different interpretations of the poem, for example *The poet thinks that the crew were kidnapped*, *Before the people disappeared life on the ship was very ordinary*. Ask the group to discuss them and, using the poem as evidence, mark on the grid whether they agree with them.

Extension and further reading

The *Puffin Book of Salt Sea Verse* edited by Charles Causley has a range of poems about the sea and life on it, including some that explore the sea as a mysterious place.

4: 1: T1: to investigate how settings and characters are built up from small details, and how the reader responds to them

story of the Mary Celeste is well known

Mary Celeste

gentle picture – no sense of anything out of the ordinary or violence

most of poem is made up of brief pictures of everyday life on ship

this verse describes ship after crew have disappeared

Only the wind sings
in the riggings,
the hull creaks a lullaby;
a sail lifts gently
like a message
pinned to a vacant sky.
The wheel turns
over bare decks,
shirts flap on a line;
only the song of the lapping waves
beats steady time…

Shirts washed and hung, beds made below, decks done, the boy stitches a torn sail.

The Captain
has a good ear for a tune;
played his child to sleep
on the ship's organ.
Now, music left,
he checks his compass,
lightly tips the wheel,
hopes for a westerly.
Clear sky, a friendly sea,
fair winds for Italy.

everything seems happy and normal

First mate,
off-duty from
the long dawn watch, begins
a letter to his wife, daydreams
of home.

The Captain's wife is late;
the child did not sleep
and breakfast has passed…
She, too, is missing home;
sits down at last to eat,
but can't quite force
the porridge down.
She swallows hard,
slices the top from her egg.

The child now sleeps, at last,
head firmly pressed into her pillow
in a deep sea-dream.

unanswered questions

Then why are the gulls wheeling
like vultures in the sky?
Why was the child snatched
from her sleep? What drew
the Captain's cry?

3 sinister events in this verse – verbs are more violent than 1st italicised verse; dramatic contrast in atmosphere between this verse and preceding ones

no one seems to have any inkling that something is about to happen

The second mate
is happy.
A four-hour sleep,
full stomach
and a quiet sea
are all he craves.
He has all three.

Only the wind replies
in the rigging,
and the hull creaks and sighs;
a sail spells out its message
over silent skies.
The wheel still turns
over bare decks,
shirts blow on the line;
the siren-song of lapping waves
still echoes over time.

last verse echoes 1st verse, but changes are significant

Judith Nicholls

in Greek mythology, sirens would lure ships to destruction with their irresistible song

4: 1: T7: to compare and contrast poems on similar themes, particularly their form and language, discussing personal responses and preferences

4: 1: T14: to write poems based on personal or imagined experience, linked to poems read

Legend

by Philip Larkin

Background

This poem, like 'Mary Celeste', focuses on a mysterious ship and its journey. It seems to be inspired initially by sea shanties and the first line is reminiscent of a Christmas carol.

Help the children to understand a *legend* as a traditional story with heroic characters, which may be based on truth, but has been embellished over the years.

Shared reading and discussing the text

● Read the poem a number of times so the children become familiar with its rhyme and rhythm. Ask them to notice something different each time, for example the rhyme scheme, the refrain, the changing adjective in the second line. Clarify the meaning of vocabulary such as *rigged*, *running*, *all possessed*.

● Ask the children to identify any legends they know (perhaps King Arthur or Robin Hood). Draw out that the poet may have called the poem 'Legend' because he is writing about something mysterious and strange. He is creating a story which might have a nugget of truth in it, but which cannot be proved to be true or false.

● Return to the text and contrast the first and second ships. Draw a simple map to illustrate the different directions the ships took. Ask the children to discuss which of the two ships had the better journey, justifying their answer.

● Now look at the third ship. Add its direction to the map. Point out the references to darkness in verses 4 and 5 – the ship seems to be sailing into a world where little can be seen. Ask individuals to mark all the references to wind. This should help them to see that the third ship is almost becalmed in a frosty, cold world. Finally explore their understanding of *unfruitful* – not only is it a dark and windless place, it seems empty of life.

● Read the final six lines again. Look for differences between the first two ships and the third one. One major difference seems to be that the third ship never comes back to port. Why does that make the last line of the poem sound ominous and mysterious? (Perhaps because it implies the ship will sail on for ever.)

Activities

● Prepare a cloze procedure omitting the adjectives in the second line of each verse. Explain to the group that you don't want them to try to remember the correct words but discuss what would fit well. Remind them that in the original the adjectives are used to make the sea sound rougher, then more ominous, as the poem goes on.

● Together, write another verse for the poem. It should follow the same rhyme scheme and use a variation on the repeated second line. Discuss where to place the new verse. For example, if it is about the third ship, would it fit best towards the end of the poem?

● Use a similarities and differences grid to collect ideas about 'Legend' and 'Mary Celeste'. Re-read and discuss them with the group. Look at features such as the amount of detail (much more in 'Mary Celeste'), the use of verbs (more varied in 'Mary Celeste'), adjectives (more in 'Legend'), rhyme, rhythm and repetition. Encourage the group to speculate why there might be these differences. (For example, in 'Legend' the poet is using adjectives to create a mysterious, threatening world.)

● Evolve a reading of the poem that brings out the mystery of the third ship and its journey. Use musical instruments to add sound effects.

Extension/further reading

Use the two poems to invent a scenario to explore through drama: A group of people are on a cliff path beside the sea, when they see a battered ship sail slowly by. The people assume it is the legendary ship that sails on for ever. What can they see from the cliff? What do they think about the ship? This drama work could be developed into written eyewitness accounts.

Otherworlds: Poems of the Mysterious compiled by Judith Nicholls (Faber & Faber) is a good collection of poems with mysterious subject matter or themes.

4: 1: T1: to investigate how settings are built up from small details, and how the reader responds to them

4: 1: T7: compare and contrast poems on similar themes, particularly their form and language, discussing personal responses and preferences

old story, the truth of which no one can be sure

sounds like a Christmas carol

1st ship had easiest voyage

2nd ship had a difficult voyage

was the ship becalmed?

seems to suggest that the ship went on sailing for ever, it never returned to port

this line has echoes in every verse

this line is echoed throughout the poem

interesting adjectives suggest how the journeys were different

at least 2nd ship returned

Legend

I saw three ships go sailing by,
Over the sea, the lifting sea,
And the wind rose in the morning sky,
And one was rigged for a long journey.

The first ship turned towards the west,
Over the sea, the running sea,
And by the wind was all possessed
And carried to a rich country.

The second turned towards the east,
Over the sea, the quaking sea,
And the wind hunted it like a beast
To anchor in captivity.

The third ship drove towards the north,
Over the sea, the darkening sea,
But no breath of wind came forth,
And the decks shone frostily.

The northern sky rose high and black
Over the proud unfruitful sea,
East and west the ships came back
Happily or unhappily:

But the third went wide and far
Into an unforgiving sea
Under a fire-spilling star,
And it was rigged for a long journey.

Philip Larkin

4: 1: T14: to write poems based on imagined experience, linked to poems read

Wind

by Dionne Brand

Background

This poem personifies a natural phenomenon. It gives the wind human characteristics and a personality through using it as the narrator, and can offer a useful writing pattern.

Shared reading and discussing the text

● Cover the title of the poem. Explain to the children that after you have read the poem you want them to tell you who *I* is. Read the poem together more than once.

● If the children cannot work out the speaker, point out the clue in *I became a breeze…*

● Once you have established the subject, explain that the poem works by imagining that the wind is a person and gives many small pictures of this wind-person in action. Ask children to identify and explain the pictures. For example, how can the wind pull a bird out of the sky? Ask what sort of person the wind seems to be. The children should be able to identify the wind's strength and naughtiness.

● Check understanding of metaphors like *cotton streamers* (clouds stretched out across the sky) and vocabulary like *guava*. Then focus on the verbs in the poem, for example *scooped.* Ask the children to work in pairs to suggest some alternative verbs with similar meanings. Collect the ideas and ask which is the most powerful. Can they suggest alternatives to the more ordinary verb *broke* in *I broke a limb…*?

● Explain that you want to write a poem where the weather is described as if it were a person. Agree a topic, such as rain, and generate vocabulary like *torrential* and *drizzle*, including appropriate dialect. Ask: *If the rain were a person, how would it behave?* Turn some ideas into lines for the poem, for example *I splatter the windows with water* '. Explain your thinking process: *I must remember to use 'I' as this is written in the first person; I must look back at that verb to check it says what I want it to say.*

Activities

● Remind the children of the poem you had modelled in shared writing and ask them to work in pairs to develop their own lines that present vivid pictures of what the rain might do. Discuss ideas and encourage children to reflect on how lines might be improved, perhaps by substituting more vivid verbs or including adjectives or adverbs.

● More able writers could be asked to work through the poetry-writing process with another weather type. They can brainstorm lists of ideas, draft sentences, think about the personality they are trying to convey, select and improve lines accordingly. Less independent writers may need the support of a writing frame, with sentence starters or question prompts, or your support through guided writing.

● Prepare a cloze procedure on 'Wind' by covering a selection of verbs. Ask children to work in pairs to suggest alternatives. Emphasise this is not a memory exercise, rather that you wish to explore interesting verbs that could be included.

● Re-read the poem written in shared and guided writing. Remind the class that Dionne Brand wrote a poem where she spoke as if she were the wind, and managed to convey a personality too. What personality would the rain have? Modify and redraft the poem to bring out this personality, for example by selecting some lines as showing rain behaving more 'in character'; by adding appropriate adjectives; and by reviewing the use of verbs.

Extension/further reading

Riddles are often written as if an object is speaking. Get a group to research riddles, for example they could look in JRR Tolkein's *The Hobbit* where Bilbo meets Gollum, and try writing their own.

Make a collection of poems that use personification, for example 'Dazzledance' by John Rice and 'Spells' by James Reeves (both in *Read Me: A Poem a Day for the National Year of Reading*, Macmillan). Let the group read them and then brainstorm ideas for a poster titled 'A good personification poem should…'.

4: 1: T14: to write poems based on personal or imagined experience, linked to poems read. List brief phrases and words, experiment by trimming or extending sentences; experiment with powerful and expressive verbs

poem presents lots of pictures of what the wind can do

Wind

'I' is used consistently throughout; the wind is speaking, it is being personified

examples of powerful verbs

rather more ordinary verb

I pulled a hummingbird out of the sky one day
   but let it go,
I heard a song and carried it with me
   on my cotton streamers,
I dropped it on an ocean and lifted up a wave
   with my bare hands,
I made a whole canefield tremble and bend
   as I ran by,
I pushed a soft cloud from here to there,
I hurried a stream along a pebbled path,
I scooped up a yard of dirt and hurled it in the air,
I lifted a straw hat and sent it flying,
I broke a limb from a guava tree,
I became a breeze, bored and tired,
and hovered and hung and rustled and lay
   where I could.

Dionne Brand

are these clouds?

the wind has great strength

the wind sounds like a naughty child

4: 1: S3: to identify the use of powerful verbs… e.g. through cloze procedures

Charlie and the Chocolate Factory: A Play

Extract 1

by Roald Dahl and Richard R George

Background

Playscripts are written in a particular format as they are intended to be acted from, not just read. Speakers are identified in the left-hand margin, stage directions and actors' instructions are briefly given, and the main body of the text is almost entirely made up of characters' words. There is usually very little description of character, and speech marks are not used.

Charlie and the Chocolate Factory is one of Roald Dahl's best-known stories. This adaptation was made for schools by Richard George, a teacher from New York. It was first performed by his class in 1973.

In the story, the greatest chocolate maker in the world, Willy Wonka, has organised a competition. Five Golden Tickets have been wrapped in five ordinary chocolate bars. Whoever finds a ticket wins a tour of Mr Wonka's factory and enough chocolate for the rest of their lives. Up to now, four tickets have been found by some rather disagreeable children. In this extract, the audience meet the hero of the story, Charlie, and his family.

Shared reading and discussing the text

● Ask if any of the children have read the story or watched it as a film. Explain that this text is an adaptation of the novel as a play.

● Read and enjoy the extract. Ask the children what they can infer about the four ticket winners. Check their understanding of the difficulties facing Charlie's family.

● Ask why the text is set out as it is. Clarify the children's understanding of the playscript format: the way names are listed, the use of the colon, no speech marks. Ensure they understand the function of stage directions.

● Re-read the narrator's words. Check understanding of the narrator as one who tells the story. Identify how he (or she) introduces the Bucket family. Look for examples where this narrator, unusually, also comments on the action, such as *I'm worried about Charlie*.

● Follow the comments about the ticket winners, up to *some nasty little beast who*

doesn't deserve it! Ask the children, in pairs, to identify what they have learned from these exchanges. Now focus on Grandpa Joe's next lines – what do they hint might happen?

● Ask the children to read Charlie's first lines as effectively as possible. Help them to appreciate that Charlie is almost weak with delight, remembering the smell of the chocolate. Can they revise their reading so that he sounds dreamy, remembering something wonderful?

● Highlight the last three lines of the scene. How is the writer preparing the audience for what might happen next?

Activities

● Ask the group to discuss and then list three things they have learned from this scene about Charlie, two about Grandpa Joe and one about the other characters. Introduce this as part of a guided reading activity to support less able readers. Encourage them to notice how the whole scene contributes to the feeling that Charlie deserves to win the last ticket.

● Ask a children to draw and label a 'knowledge line', to chart what they know at the start of the scene and what they have learned by the end. You could make the task easier by identifying which parts of the text they should focus on.

● Ask the children to work out an oral reading. They should first note how to read particular lines, then read the text aloud, either to a friend who comments on their interpretation, or into a tape recorder so that they can review their work and make changes if necessary.

● Act out the extract. Ask children to try different actions linked to what the characters say. How will they make the grandparents look and sound different from each other? What extra stage directions would the children add?

Extension and further reading

In guided writing, children could adapt a scene from another novel into a playscript. Extracts with a lot of dialogue are easier than descriptive ones. Ask them to use a narrator to fill in essential information that the audience need.

4: 1: T1: to investigate how characters are built up from small details, and how the reader responds to them

4: 1: T5: to prepare, read and perform playscripts; compare organisation of scripts with stories

no speech marks used

narrator, unusually, directly addresses the audience and makes comments

layout is characteristic of playscripts:

1. stage directions centred and in brackets and italic

2. small caps with colon for characters

3. indented text

stage directions enable us to imagine how the play would be performed – instructions to actors and director

Extract 1

CHARLIE AND THE CHOCOLATE FACTORY: A PLAY

NARRATOR: I almost forgot… this is our hero – Charlie Bucket. Charlie's a nice boy. Of course he's been starving lately. In fact the whole family has. I'm worried about Charlie, though. Why, did you know that Charlie is so weak from not eating that he walks slowly instead of running like the other kids, so he can save his energy? Well, I've said far too much already. Let's find out what's happening at the Bucket house now… uhh, I'll see you later.

[NARRATOR *exits.* BUCKET FAMILY *comes to life*]

MR BUCKET: Well, I see that four children have found Golden Tickets. I wonder who the fifth lucky person will be?

GRANDMA JOSEPHINE: I hope it's no one like that repulsive Gloop boy!

GRANDPA GEORGE: As spoiled as that Veruca Salt girl!

GRANDMA GEORGINA: Or as beastly as that bubble-popping Violet Beauregarde!

MRS BUCKET: Or living such a useless life as that Teavee boy!

MR BUCKET [*Looking up from his paper*]: It makes you wonder if all children behave like this nowadays… like these brats we've been hearing about.

GRANDPA JOE: Of course not! Some do, of course. In fact, quite a lot of them do. But not all.

MRS BUCKET: And now there's only one ticket left.

GRANDMA JOSEPHINE: Quite so… and just as sure as I'll be having cabbage soup for supper tomorrow, that ticket'll go to some nasty little beast who doesn't deserve it!

GRANDPA JOE: I bet I know somebody who'd like to find a Golden Ticket. How about it, Charlie? You love chocolate more than anyone I ever saw!

CHARLIE: Yes, I sure would, Grandpa Joe! You know… it just about makes me faint when I have to pass Mr Wonka's Chocolate Factory every day as I go to school. The smell of that wonderful chocolate makes me so dreamy that I often fall asleep and bump into Mr Wonka's fence. But I guess I should realize that dreams don't come true. Just imagine! Me imagining that I could win the fifth Golden Ticket. Why, it's… it's… it's pure imagination.

GRANDPA JOE: Well my boy, it may be pure imagination, but I've heard tell that what you imagine sometimes comes true.

CHARLIE: Gee, you really think so, Grandpa Joe? Gee… I wonder…

End of Scene 2

succinct, descriptive adjectives

names say a lot about the children's characters

lots of information about competition

she has a very low opinion of some children

sets up possibility that Charlie might win the last ticket

chocolate factory has an amazing effect on Charlie

very American expression

we are being prepared for what might happen

4: 1: T6: to chart the build-up of a play scene, e.g. how scenes start, how dialogue is expressed, and how scenes are concluded

4: 1: T13: to write playscripts, e.g. using known stories as a basis

Charlie and the Chocolate Factory: A Play

Extract 2

by Roald Dahl and Richard R George

Background
This text continues from the point reached in the last extract. The Bucket family are discussing Charlie and the competition.

Shared reading and discussing the text
● Remind the children of the previous extract. Ask what the Bucket family thought of the children who had won Golden Tickets so far. What had Grandpa Joe said to encourage Charlie to hope that he might win a ticket? Remind them too of the technical language of plays, such as *narrator, stage direction.*

● Read the extract a number of times. After a couple of readings, ask for volunteers to read parts aloud, or ask children to read the extract in pairs, alternating roles. Ask for comments about how particular lines ought to be read.

● Point out the stage directions *running in excitedly* (line 20) and *excitedly* (line 26). Ask why they are written in italic. What information do these stage directions give? Explain that they tell the actor something about how the lines should be said and what feelings should be shown. Point out too that they are both adverbs, and that many adverbs end in *ly.*

● Distinguish between *running in excitedly* and *excitedly.* In the first example, the adverb adds detail to the verb *running.* In the second, the verb is implied or suggested and applies to the character's speech. Take suggestions for the 'missing' verb.

● Ask the children to think of other adverbs that could indicate how characters speak. They could use an adverbial phrase, such as *quietly but happily* or just an adverb: *sadly, happily.* Add suggestions to the text on Post-it Notes.

● Re-read the text again. Notice that Charlie's final speech breaks off. Point out how this is presented through ellipses, the repetition of *and* and broken sentences. The writer is deliberately slowing the action to build suspense and highlight the characters' excitement.

● Ask the children to predict what Charlie might say next. Explain that he is building up to telling his family that he has found the Golden Ticket. He doesn't tell them immediately, perhaps because he is in shock and out of breath. How could he further delay telling the news? (He tells them that he found 50p, went to the shop, bought one chocolate bar, and then another. It was in the second bar that he found the ticket.) Together, write the next part of the scene, using the children's ideas.

Activities
● Ask children to plan the next part of the scene. They should start where the extract finishes, and include three delays before Charlie reveals that he has found the Golden Ticket. They could use a planning sheet like this:

What Charlie says	How the others react
And I couldn't believe my eyes	
Delay 1 –	
Delay 2 –	
Delay 3 –	
And it was there I found the Golden Ticket	

Encourage them to make the delays as imaginative and interesting as possible. As they begin to write, remind them to put in comments from the other characters, expressing excitement, impatience, disappointment and so on. For a less able group, give them a template to help organise their writing as a play.

● Use the hot-seating technique to interview the characters and find out their thoughts, hopes and concerns at this point in the story. Afterwards, discuss which answers were plausible and understandable in the light of what you have read so far. Less confident children could prepare questions in advance.

Extension and further reading
Ask an able group to collect examples of American vocabulary used in both extracts and prepare an English–American glossary for presentation to the class.

Compare this extract with the version of the scene in the novel and, if possible, with the film version available on video.

4: 1: T4: to explore narrative order: identify build-ups

4: 1: T5: to prepare, read and perform playscripts; compare organisation of scripts with stories

---

Extract 2

CHARLIE AND THE CHOCOLATE FACTORY: A PLAY

SCENE 3

Bucket home, several days later. **GRANDPARENTS, MR** and **MRS BUCKET,** *as before.*

MR BUCKET: You know, it sure would have been nice if Charlie had won that fifth Golden Ticket.

MRS BUCKET: You mean with that 10p we gave him for his birthday present yesterday?

MR BUCKET: Yes, the one we gave him to buy the one piece of candy he gets every year.

GRANDMA GEORGINA: And just think how long it took you two to save that 10p.

GRANDPA GEORGE: Yes, now that was really a shame.

GRANDMA JOSEPHINE: But think of how Charlie enjoyed the candy. He just loves Willy Wonka chocolate.

MRS BUCKET: He didn't really *act* that disappointed.

MR BUCKET: No, he didn't —

GRANDPA JOE: Well, he might not have acted disappointed, but that's because he's a fine boy and wouldn't want any of us to feel sorry for him. Why – what boy wouldn't be disappointed? I sure wish he'd won. I'd do anything for that boy. Why I'd even —

CHARLIE [*Running in excitedly*]: Mum! Dad! Grandpa Joe! Grandfolks! You'll never believe it! You'll never believe what happened!

MRS BUCKET: Good gracious, Charlie – what happened?

CHARLIE: Well… I was walking home… and the wind was so cold… and the snow was blowing so hard… and I couldn't see where I was going… and I was looking down to protect my face… and… and —

MR BUCKET [*Excitedly*]: Go on, Charlie… go on, Charlie… what is it?

CHARLIE: And there it was… just lying there in the snow… kind of buried… and I looked around… and no one seemed to look as if they had lost anything… and… and… and so I picked it up and wiped it off… and I couldn't believe my eyes —

implies that they cannot afford to give him very much at all

example of American idiom –'sweets'/'chocolate'

yet this is English

repetition of ellipsis and 'and' shows Charlie is too shocked and excited to speak properly

Charlie seems to enlarge the difficulties he faces

poverty of Bucket family is exaggerated for comic effect (typical Roald Dahl feature)

gives information to actor about how to interpret lines

Charlie is building up to announcing something important; the vital information is being delayed

---

4: 1: T6: to chart the build-up of a play scene, e.g. how scenes start, how dialogue is expressed, and how scenes are concluded

4: 1: T13: to write playscripts, e.g. using known stories as basis

4: 1: S4: to identify adverbs and understand their function in sentences through identifying common adverbs with *ly* suffix and discussing their impact on the meaning of sentences

Hero worship

Background

This extract is taken from a section of the *Funday Times*, a children's newspaper. This article was published in Spring 2002, shortly before *Spider-Man* was released in the UK.

This feature article includes typical elements of newspaper form, including a headline that plays on words, a summary opening paragraph and the use of quotes from an interview.

Shared reading and discussing the text

● Discuss with the children what they know about Spider-Man and other superheroes. Ask what is so special about a superhero. Allow the children to talk about their answers in pairs or groups first, to encourage less confident children to contribute. Establish that superheroes often have unnatural strength and special powers and that they fight evil wherever they find it. Explain that Spider-Man, unlike most superheroes lives in a real place. Now read the first two paragraphs of the article.

● Tell the children that this text is from a newspaper. Ask them to identify any features characteristic of newspapers, for example a bold headline.

● Point out and mark other features that stand out, such as the pun in *snares the UK in its web*. Ask the children to explain why this is a clever use of language. (It is a metaphor – like a spider catches a fly, the UK is being caught in the enthusiasm for the film.)

● Another feature of newspaper writing is the use of colloquial language or language that is quite close to speech, for example *chats*.

● Discuss whether the opening paragraph makes the children want to read on. As well as having an interesting subject matter, is the opening presented in a way that entices them to read more? Explain that the opening sentences are very important in a newspaper or magazine – they must grab a reader's attention or the article won't be read.

● Read the rest of the text. Point out that it introduces the subject (Stan Lee) and then quotes from an interview with him. Explain that

quotes like this are another characteristic of newspaper or magazine writing. Ask the children what they have found out about him from the article. Did any of the children already know any of the character's origins?

● Go back to the opening two paragraphs. Discuss the difference between fact and opinion. Which words, phrases and sentences do the children know or assume to be true? (The movie arrives on June 14th.) Which are the writer's opinions? (Some people may not agree that a comic-strip character is *humble*.) Now ask them to find other examples of fact and opinion in the text. How could they check whether something was a fact or opinion? (Discuss the use of information books, encyclopedias, the Internet, other newspapers.)

Activities

● Give the group the whole text and a set of highlighter pens. Remind them of the different features of newspaper reports or articles: headline, lead or summary paragraph, quotes and so on. Ask the children to find these in the text, marking them in different colours. What is left unmarked? Help the children to identify that it is background material about the cartoons and their creator.

● Ask the group to cut out the headline and first few sentences or lead paragraphs from similar types of articles in other papers. Analyse the features of the examples collected.

● Evolve catchy headlines for articles on ordinary subjects, for example 'School band hits the right note!'. Using the text, remind the children of the features of effective article openings and encourage them to experiment with puns, unexpected verbs and an enthusiastic tone, as well as being aware of their audience.

Extension/further reading

Make a dictionary of colloquial phrases that are used today, such as *cool* as discussed in the text and compared to *groovy*. Ask children to take their dictionary list home and research comparative phrases that their parents used.

4: 1: T16: to identify different types of text, e.g. their content, structure, vocabulary, style, layout and purpose

4: 1: T18: to select and examine opening sentences that capture interest, etc.; pick out key sentences that convey information

4: 1: T19: to understand and use the terms *fact* and *opinion*; and to begin to distinguish the two in reading and other media

headline – very important in newspaper articles and reports for grabbing attention

puns are typical of newspapers

Hero worship

As Spider-Man fever snares the UK in its web, Buzz! takes a look at the original cartoon superhero and chats to his creator, Stan Lee.

opening paragraph acts as a kind of summary introduction

colloquial language

One of this summer's big action blockbusters – the record-breaking new Spider-Man movie – arrives in the UK on June 14, but like most superheroes, the crime-fighting webmaster began life as a humble comic-strip character.

superheroes have unnatural strength and special powers

Spider-Man creator Stan Lee grew up during an exciting era when the superheroes of today, such as Superman and Batman, were in their comic book prime. Unlike other superheroes, Stan Lee was keen for his creation to live in the real world as it produced more believable and engaging stories.

simple cartoon drawing compared to the special-effects-laden, 3-D version of the new film

"I lived In New York and Marvel Comics was also in New York, so it was easy for me to write the stories if I set them in New York too," Stan explains. "Spider-Man had a real address, he lived in Forrest Hills – and there is a Forrest Hills. He didn't live in Smallville or Gotham City."

article is put together with direct quotations and commentary

Stan had already made his name creating the Fantastic Four, and was eager to continue with his comic book inventions. "After I finished the Fantastic Four, I wanted to create a story with just one hero and I thought, what super-power can I give him?" he recalls.

"As you can imagine, the super-power is the key to the whole thing." But what attributes would Stan select to make his new hero a superhero?

one of the distinguishing features of Spider-Man – he lives in a real place

interesting that it was a fly, not a spider, that seems to be the original inspiration

"I thought to myself, we already have somebody who is very strong, we have characters that can fly, what can I do?" Stan explains. "I saw a fly crawling up the wall and thought: 'Wouldn't it be cool to have somebody who can crawl up a wall?'... except I probably didn't say: 'Wouldn't it be cool' – because that was so many years ago. I said: 'Wouldn't it be groovy!'"

4: 1: T20: to identify the main features of newspapers, including layout, range of information, voice, level of formality; organisation of articles, advertisements and headlines

They all kept on running

Background

This extract is taken from an article in the twice-weekly *Whitby Gazette* in October 2002. It refers to the Great North Run and Junior Run which took place the previous weekend.

The text contrasts with the extract from the *Funday Times*, since it is not written specifically for children and is in traditional newspaper report style rather than being an editorial or magazine-style article.

Shared reading and discussing the text

● Cover the text except for the headline. Ask what sort of text this line is from. How can the children tell? Discuss the use of headlines as a kind of summary of the article, intended to catch the reader's attention. Then ask what the text might be about. Point out the clue in the word *running*. Make a note of the predictions.

● Uncover the first two paragraphs. Do they confirm the children's prediction? Can they now be more specific when explaining what the text is about? Explain that newspapers usually use the first few sentences of an article – the lead paragraph – as a summary of the whole story. Also point out that each of the paragraphs is just a single sentence – this too is a characteristic of newspaper writing.

● Now read the rest of the extract. Tell the children that the report is from a local rather than a national newspaper. Ask what difference that makes to the focus of the story. For example, there is nothing about the winner of the race, but lots about local people, places and schools. Ask volunteers to highlight lines that mention people or places which someone from Whitby might be interested in, but which might mean very little to anyone else.

● Go back to the second paragraph and ask the children if they can find two facts. Point out the verb *enjoyed*. Is this also a fact? Explain that actually this is the reporter's opinion or interpretation – it is impossible to prove that all 7000 runners enjoyed the race. Do the same with the paragraph beginning *Alec Duffield (14)…* Ask the children to underline the facts in

one colour, and the word that signals an opinion (*amazing*) in another.

Activities

● Model how to write a newspaper report about a class or school event. Explain that the title or headline is often decided on last, so you will begin with one or two opening sentences that summarise the whole article. Then, or in a subsequent lesson, move into the detail of the story. Like this extract, use names of people and places to make it interesting. Model how to use adjectives and verbs to introduce your interpretation about the events described. When the piece is complete, re-read and decide together on an appropriate headline.

● Ask the children to write their own article or report about a local issue or event. Split the writing into two phases, the first to concentrate on the writing of the opening sentence or two, the second to give the detail of the report and add the headline. As a more challenging activity, set constraints on the report, for example allowing them only five short paragraphs or 150 words to tell the story.

● Word-process the articles written and encourage children to edit them on screen, for example adapting the headline, converting the text into columns. Encourage them to experiment with newspaper layouts.

● Ask the children to mark factual information in the text in one colour and adjectives and verbs that show the reporter's opinion in another. (There are a number of opinions in the last third of the article.)

● Find a report on a road race, such as the Great North Run or London Marathon from a national newspaper to compare with this text. Once you have discussed them, you might ask the children to list similarities and differences.

Extension/further reading

Find an article from the paper that is local to the school, relevant to the interests of the children. Analyse it together to find out whether the same features are apparent.

4: 1: T18: to select and examine opening sentences that set scenes, capture interest, etc.; pick out key sentences that convey information

4: 1: T19: to understand and use the terms *fact* and *opinion*; and to begin to distinguish the two in reading

4: 1: T20: to identify the main features of newspapers, including layout, range of information, voice, level of formality; organisation of articles, and headlines

headline summarises the article and encourages the reader to read on

report is from a local paper, gives a local perspective on a national event

lead paragraph gives an overview of whole article

single-sentence paragraphs

notice how many times the word 'local' is used

They all kept on running to raise cash for charities

DOZENS of runners from the Whitby area were among the thousands who took part in the great North Run in Gateshead recently.

Locals of all ages enjoyed the 13.1 mile road race through the streets of Gateshead and Newcastle.

Many were raising money for local good causes or their favourite charities.

And local student Alec Duffield finished in the top ten of the BUPA Junior Great North Fun Run, which a total of 7,000 students took part in on the day before the main run itself.

Here is a look at some of our local competitors and how they fared…

❑ Seventy Eskdale School students (including eight year 10s who transferred from Eskdale to Whitby Community College in September) and thirty parents travelled to Gateshead for the Junior Great North Run. Over 7,000 students participated. Everyone enjoyed the new route which took in the Quayside and the new Millennium Bridge.

Alec Duffield (14) this year came ninth in an amazing time of 1 hour 16 minutes 50 seconds! Mrs Landers (teacher in charge of the library) and Mrs Dixon (the librarian) both ran the course. (Mrs Dixon also ran in Sunday's adult race.)

Esk Valley Coaches (formerly Procters) helped the school by providing coaches at a reduced price, so that all sponsor money collected will go towards purchasing the new microlibrarian system for the school library (whereby students are issued books through a fingerprint recognition system), and Leukaemia Research. The school are hoping to raise approximately £1,500.

Several children from East Whitby Primary School also ran, so there was a real "community feel" to the day.

❑ Siblings Mollie (8) and Charlie (5) Smith raised £200 for Helredale Play Centre funds when they took part in the junior race.

They were delighted to meet ex-boxer and pantomime veteran Frank Bruno and also enjoyed a post-race concert staged by S Club Juniors.

The pair, who live in Whitby, will get to choose what equipment they would like to spend the money on.

lots of proper nouns

fact

opinion expressed through an adjective

unusual choice of verb – an opinion rather than a fact

local school is a special focus of this article

nothing about the winner because he was not local!

4: 1: T24: to write newspaper style reports, e.g. about school events or an incident from a story, including:
● composing headlines
● using IT to draft and lay out reports
● editing stories to fit a particular space
● organising writing into paragraphs

Seven feared dead in space shuttle disaster

Background

This report is from the website of the *Guardian* newspaper, about the destruction of the Columbia spacecraft in February 2003. The article includes some characteristic features of newspaper reports, such as the headline, quotes from an eyewitness and an opening paragraph that briefly summarises the subject.

Shared reading and discussing the text

● Discuss what, if anything, the children can recall about the Columbia disaster. Explain what a space shuttle is and what it is used for.

● Work with the class on a KWL grid, completing the K and W sections. A KWL grid is a means of recording what is known at the start of a piece of research; identifying what is to be found out; and what has been learned when the research has been completed:

K	W	L
What I **know** about the explosion of the Columbia space shuttle	What I **want** to find out	What I have **learned**

Discuss with the children what they already know about the accident and note their ideas in the K column. Ask what they would like to find out and record these as questions in the W column. Explain that reading the report may provide some of the answers, but they may need to do more research to complete their table, for example into developments in the investigation into the cause.

● Now read through the article. Ask the children if any of their questions have been answered. Add information to the L column of the table. Ask if they have learned anything else from the article, which they had not expected.

● Re-read the text. Ask the children if they can tell what sort of text it is, perhaps pointing out the date as a clue. Identify the newspaper-like features, including the use of headline, byline, summary opening paragraph, short paragraphs, eyewitness accounts and quotes from local residents and the authorities. Mark these on the text. Help the children to appreciate too the formal tone and the authoritative voice.

● Ask the children to find clues that indicate the report was written soon after the accident. (The date, the shuttle *appears* to have broken up, that Nasa had *not yet confirmed* events, government officials were *awaiting updates*.)

Activities

● Ask groups to update the story by researching what scientists now believe to have caused the accident to Columbia. Add any relevant information to the KWL grid.

● Ask more able children to investigate what has happened to space exploration and shuttle flights since the Columbia accident. Set them a question to research, for example: *How has the Columbia accident change America's space programme?* They should use a KWL grid to organise their ideas and direct their questions.

● Compare a newspaper report from the *Guardian* or its website (www.guardian.co.uk) with one on the same topic written explicitly for children, for example CBBC's *Newsround* website (www.bbc.co.uk/cbbcnews). Develop a similarities and differences chart. (It is likely that although facts will be similar in both stories, there will be differences in presentation, use of language and depth of detail.)

● Using current information about the Columbia accident and its possible causes, work with a group to rewrite the report, updating it for today. Discuss which elements will be the same (because the basic information hasn't changed) and which aspects will need amending in the light of the new information.

Extension/further reading

Compare a news item on the *Newsround* television programme with the version on the programme's website. Talk about what effect the use of pictures and live material has on the way that the story is told.

4: 1: T20: to identify the main features of newspapers, including layout, range of information, voice, level of formality; organisation of articles and headlines

4: 1: T21: to predict newspaper stories from the evidence of headlines, making notes and then checking against the original

headline is an obvious clue that extract is from a news report; typical 'shorthand' style of wording – only essential words included, no 'are', 'a', 'the' and so on

newspaper reports often have multiple authors or contributors

date and non-specific language of byline indicate report was written soon after the accident happened

opening paragraph summarises whole of report, giving key information that will be expanded on later

this phrase also shows report was written very soon after accident; details are not yet certain

Seven feared dead in space shuttle disaster

Staff and agencies
Saturday February 1, 2003

The space shuttle Columbia appears to have broken up in flames over North Texas. It is feared that all seven crew members, six Americans and an Israeli, have been killed.

The American space agency Nasa said that all communications were lost as the shuttle was flying at approximately 12,500 miles per hour, just 16 minutes before it was due to land at the Kennedy space centre. The space agency has not yet confirmed the fate of the shuttle but plans to issue a further public statement shortly.

Local residents in North Texas have reported hearing a 'big bang' similar to a sonic boom and seeing debris falling to the ground, leading to growing fears that the shuttle had broken up on re-entry.

Gary Hunziker in Plano, Texas, said he saw the shuttle flying overhead. "I could see two bright objects flying off each side of it. I just assumed they were chase jets."

"The barn started shaking and we ran out and started looking around," said Benjamin Laster of Kemp, Texas. "I saw a puff of vapour and smoke and saw a big chunk of metal fall."

Nasa warned people on the ground in Texas to stay away from any fallen debris.

President George W. Bush was informed of the situation. Bush administration officials said that they were awaiting updates from Nasa and that they had no immediate information that terrorism was involved. Security had been extraordinarily tight for Columbia's 16-day scientific research mission because of the presence of Ilan Ramon, the first Israeli astronaut.

This was the 113th flight in the shuttle program's 22 years and the 28th flight for Columbia, Nasa's oldest shuttle. It is the second space shuttle disaster in 16 years, following the loss of the Challenger space shuttle in January 1986.

quotations from eyewitnesses lend authenticity and a personal view

single-sentence paragraph characteristic of newspaper reports

report's formal, authoritative tone of voice is reinforced by use of numbers which suggests precision and accuracy

4: 1: T24: to write newspaper style reports

Riding on difficult surfaces

by Janet Cook

Background

This extract is from a book called *Mountain Bikes*. It is an instructional text: it tells the reader how to do something. You might discuss other instructional texts within the children's experience, for example recipes. Instructional texts usually begin with a statement of what is to be achieved and what materials are needed, before outlining a number of steps towards achieving the goal. The use of imperatives and chronological order are characteristic features.

Shared reading and discussing the text

● Before reading the text, ask for comments on the layout. Can the children identify differences between this text and a story? Help them to notice features such as sub-headings, numbered steps, bullet points, text in boxes.

● Tell the children that this extract comes from a book about mountain biking and read the title of the extract. Ask them to suggest what information they would expect on this page. What readers did the author have in mind?

● Read the first paragraph. Explain that in instructional writing we are usually told what we can do if we follow the instructions. Identify and discuss the key sentence in this introduction. (*However, you do need to…*)

● Read the section on crossing water. Point out that the first two sentences give an overview of what has to be done. Ask about the numbered points – what do they add? (They give step by step and very specific guidance.)

● Discuss why this part of the text uses numbers. (The numbered points take the rider through the action in order.) Then get the class to highlight the verbs that introduce each of the numbered points. Explain that these verbs are written in the imperative form: the language of orders and commands. See if they can think of other imperatives (such as *stop, run, ask*). Can they find the other verb written in the imperative in this part of the text? (*Lean.*)

● Discuss why imperatives are a characteristic of instructional writing and ask the children why there is not much additional information.

● Now read the section 'Before the crossing'. Can the children suggest why this part of the text is presented in a box? Can they identify features in this section that they have already discussed, such as a numbered list, imperative verbs? Point out the bullet points and explain their function – another way of organising information so that it is brief and stands out.

● Remind the children that when they began reading the extract they made a prediction regarding what they would find out. Ask them to discuss how accurate this was. They also identified a particular audience for the extract. Were they right? How do they know?

Activities

● Ask the group to translate either of the sections with numbered steps into a series of labelled diagrams that give the instructions in sequence. You might provide a format for this and talk about the use of stylised diagrams or simple drawings to convey messages simply.

● Write a leaflet on how to ride a bike. Remind the group of the features of instructional writing. Tell them to agree the information or instructions they want to include and then help them to compose it, using sub-headings, imperatives, numbered lists and so on.

● Give the children other examples of instructional writing to review features in common with this text. Using a simple grid, with the features of instructional writing down the first column, the children could simply tick features that are present in the other examples.

● One of the elements missing from this extract is a list of materials or equipment that the rider might need. (It was discussed earlier in the book.) Ask the children to re-read the text carefully and list what equipment a rider would need to follow these instructions.

Extension/further reading

Demonstrate a simple series of actions to the children and ask them to write the instructions someone could follow to do the activity.

4: 1: T22: to identify features of instructional texts including
- noting the intended outcome at the beginning
- listing materials or ingredients
- clearly set out sequential stages
- language of commands, e.g. imperative verbs

title gives an indication of the subject matter

Riding on difficult surfaces

Mountain bikes are designed to cope with extreme conditions, including water, mud, sand, ice and snow. However, you do need to adapt your riding technique in order to stay in control of your bike in these conditions. Below are some tips on how to do this.

instructional text that tells you how to do something

sub-headings

numbered steps

questions act as a kind of checklist

bullet points

boxes separate these parts of the text and make them stand out

imperative verbs – language of orders and commands

Before the crossing

♦ Inspect the stream carefully:

1. How deep is it? If it's higher than your bottom bracket, you'll end up swimming rather than riding through it.

2. Are there many boulders? If so, try to find a smoother part of the stream.

3. Is the current strong? If so, don't risk it.

♦ Lower the seat of your bike. This will make you more stable.

♦ Loosen your toe straps. You may need to remove your feet in a hurry if you lose your balance.

♦ Make sure all the nuts and bolts are done up tightly.

Crossing water

The secret of crossing shallow streams and creeks is to pedal extra hard so you keep going at a fast speed. Your momentum will then carry you over rocks and other obstacles in your way.

1. Approach the stream as quickly as possible. Lean forwards as you enter.

2. Transfer your weight to the back of the bike. This makes it easier for the front wheel to get over rocks and so on.

3. Keep pedalling all the way through if you can. This will help you keep your balance and momentum.

4. Keep your weight over the back wheel as the front wheel climbs out of the stream.

4: 1: T25: to write clear instructions using conventions learned from reading

4: 1: T26: to improve the cohesion of written instructions and directions through the use of link phrases and organisational devices such as sub-headings and numbering

Mud, snow, sand and ice
by Janet Cook

Background

This is the second extract from *Mountain Bikes*. In the original, this was included on a double page spread with the previous extract.

As it stands, this is a slightly unusual instructional text, as it is presented in tabular form and offers advice. Nevertheless, the preparation and riding tips columns both demonstrate characteristic features of the genre.

Shared reading and discussing the text

● Less able readers would benefit from guided reading of this text prior to shared work.

● Explain to the children that this text may be different from many other instructions they have seen as it is presented in a table. Model how to read a table, pointing out the significance of the column and row headings to organise material. Explain that in the column headed 'Potential Problems' the reader should find information about difficulties a rider might face. Discuss what information they expect to find in the other columns.

● Now look at the rows. What would they find in each of the rows? (Information on the impact the specific weather condition has on riding.) Demonstrate how to read the rows against the columns, showing how the table lets the reader identify specific problems and the preparation needed. Involve the children in reading across a row by asking questions that encourage recall of literal information, for example *What are some of the difficulties of riding on sand?* Point out how the information in each row is slightly different, although there is some overlap. Then ask why it is useful to present information like this. (It means that if you are planning to ride on ice, for example, you can quickly find the information you need.)

● Explain that although this text is set out in a table, many of the usual features of instructions are included. Ask the children to find examples of headings, bullet points, imperative verbs, short sentences.

● Model how to write an instructional text in

table format. Use the same column headings as in the extract, but editing 'Riding tips' to 'Tips'. Explain that the subject is *walking*, and discuss potential problems associated with it. Brainstorm ideas for row headings, for example 'Walking in the dark', 'Walking along a busy road'. Take one row heading and model how to complete each column. Encourage the children to contribute ideas (see below). As you write, 'think aloud', explaining your writing choices. Highlight the use of the features such as bullet points, imperative verbs, very short sentences.

	Potential problems	Preparation	Tips
Walking in the dark	You are not easily visible to drivers.	Wear clothing that is bright or light-reflective.	Walk at the far side, away from the kerb.

Activities

● Work with a group to complete another row for the table on walking. Encourage them to collect their ideas for each column by talking in pairs, and then discuss how to express them. As you complete a column, discuss what has been done. Highlight important elements of the writing and encourage the group to make any amendments before moving on.

● Provide a table format for the children to write an instructional piece on crossing the road, intended for younger children. Remind them of the process of identifying row headings and ask them to list some ideas for potential problems, preparation and tips. Then they should work individually to create their own tables.

Extension/further reading

Children could use the table format to write a set of instructions on any topic they are familiar with, such as playing a game, cooking, making a model.

Making Robot Warriors from Junk by Stephen Munzer (Chicken House) gives instructions on making robots in a fun and accessible way.

4: 1: T22: to identify features of instructional texts including:
- noting the intended outcome at the beginning
- listing materials or ingredients
- clearly set out sequential stages
- language of commands, e.g. imperative verbs

4: 1: T25: to write clear instructions using conventions learned from reading

Mud, snow, sand and ice

Riding on these treacherous surfaces requires a lot of common sense. In particular, keep away from melting ice, and avoid cycling in deep snow (10cm or 4ins is about the limit). Also, never cycle on these surfaces if there are other vehicles present: they could easily lose control and skid into you.

Make sure you clean your bike thoroughly afterwards.

table format makes for easy cross-referencing; columns and rows organise information; headings indicate what is included

column headings

row headings

bullet points

	Potential Problems	Preparation	Riding tips
Mud and snow	◆ Riding fast enough to avoid sinking. ◆ Steering. ◆ Skidding when climbing. ◆ Mud clogging up parts or gear cables freezing.	◆ Protect your eyes with fitted glasses. ◆ Use knobbly tyres inflated to about 35 psi. ◆ Take spray lubricant. It may help free frozen gears.	◆ Pedal quickly in a low gear. ◆ Break very gently. ◆ Steer smoothly. An abrupt turn will cause the front wheel to plough sideways.
Sand	◆ Sand on the chain makes it hard to change gear. ◆ Sinking. ◆ Sand flying in your face.	◆ Wear glasses, and wrap a scarf around your face. ◆ Don't alter tyre pressure or tread; no tyres grip sand.	◆ Stay in a low gear to avoid sinking. ◆ Steer very gently. ◆ Distribute your weight evenly across the bike.
Ice	◆ Skidding. ◆ Parts freezing up. ◆ Falling off can cause serious injury. Avoid cycling in ice if possible.	◆ Use spray lubricant on frozen parts. ◆ Neither tyre pressure nor grip make a difference.	◆ Go just fast enough to balance. ◆ No abrupt moves. ◆ If you skid, steer into the skid.

very short sentences

'pounds per square inch'

imperative verbs

some elements of overlap, as some problems occur in more than one circumstance

4: 1: T26: to improve the cohesion of written instructions and directions through the use of link phrases and organisational devices such as sub-headings and numbering

4: 1: S1: to re-read own writing to check for grammatical sense (coherence) and accuracy (agreement); to identify errors and to suggest alternative constructions

Robin Hood

Background

This report of Robin Hood from the *Oxford Children's Encyclopedia* summarises the legend, gives the known historical facts, and briefly retells one story – the outlaw's death. Compare this with the extracts from *The Outlaw Robin Hood* by Julian Atterton (see pages 10 and 12).

Reports describe the way things are or were. They tend to open with a general account of the subject and give more detailed, often technical, information in subsequent paragraphs. Reports are usually written in the present tense, are non-chronological (they don't use time connectives to organise the writing), and focus on the general rather than the specific.

Shared reading and discussing the text

● Introduce the text and relate it to the Robin Hood story looked at earlier. Explain that the extract is an encyclopedia entry. What differences would the children expect between the story and an information text? Compile a list, prompting them to say something about content and layout.

● Read the text and revisit this list. How many differences are there? Did the children notice any other features? Highlight elements such as sub-headings and inclusion of dates/facts.

● Clarify vocabulary such as *medieval, minstrel, clergymen*. Can the children define them using the sense of the text? Check meanings in a dictionary.

● Draw attention to parts of the text in inverted commas. Explain that they are well-known and often-used phrases or terms, but they are not necessarily accurate.

● Check the children's understanding of the passage, particularly the second, dense paragraph. Question them, for example *How do we know that the legend of Robin Hood was popular by 1500?* and encourage discussion. Set time limits to the discussion or ask for two reasons, where appropriate. On other occasions, give them the answer to a question, and ask them to find the evidence to support it.

● Focus on the final section. Can the children find clues that tell the reader that there is to be a story summary within the text? Highlight *A legend says* and *The story goes*. Discuss how such phrases signpost what is coming next. Can they find other phrases in the text that raise the reader's expectations? (For example, *The first written record*.) Point out that the first words in a paragraph in a text like this often have the function of introducing new information.

● Together plan an additional paragraph about Robin and Little John to include in the encyclopedia. Use the extracts from *The Outlaw Robin Hood* to recall important details about Little John and add other known information. Remind the children of how to use the opening sentence to signal to the reader what is coming, for example *One of the most famous stories about Robin tells of how he met Little John.* Ask where the drafted paragraph should be placed in the text and why.

Activities

● Ask the children to list other questions they might have about Robin Hood, which are not answered here. They should then research the answers to their questions in other information sources.

● The group could write an information paragraph about Little John. Their starting point might be the 'signpost' sentence composed in shared writing. Support less confident writers by agreeing the information to include and how to organise their paragraph.

● Re-read the text, then ask the group to summarise the passage into five bullet points that focus on the most important information. Help less able writers to draw five pictures to represent key information and write brief explanatory captions for each.

Extension/further reading

There is an interesting account of how a modern author used historical sources to retell the stories in Robert Leeson's *The Story of Robin Hood* (Kingfisher).

4: 1: T17: to identify features of non-fiction texts in print and IT, e.g. headings, lists, bullet points, captions which support the reader in gaining information efficiently

4: 1: T26: to improve the cohesion of text through the use of link phrases and organisational devices such as sub-headings and numbering

Robin Hood

According to legend, Robin Hood was an outlaw who lived in Sherwood Forest, Nottinghamshire. He 'stole from the rich and gave to the poor'. Among the 'merry men' who followed him were Little John, Friar Tuck and Will Scarlet. There might have been a real medieval person called Robin Hood, but the legend was probably based on the adventures of several real outlaws, in both Sherwood Forest and Barnsdale Forest, Yorkshire.

The first written record of Robin comes from the 1370s. Travelling minstrels had been spreading his legend for many years before then. By about 1450 Robin Hood plays were being put on. And by 1500 men were dressing up as Robin Hood in May Day games, accompanied by girls dressed as 'Maid Marion', the love of the outlaw's life. Over the centuries descriptions of Robin often changed. But he was always seen as a good Christian, as an enemy of wicked local officials and corrupt clergymen, as a great archer and swordsman, and as a master of disguise. ■

The death of Robin Hood
A legend says that Robin was bled to death by the Prioress of Kirklee Priory, who pretended she was trying to heal him. The story goes that when Robin Hood lay dying, he summoned Little John by blowing his horn three times. When Little John came to him, Robin fired an arrow into the air and asked Little John that he be buried wherever it landed, beneath the greenwood trees.

sub-heading

paragraphs are introduced by key phrases

these phrases signal a story summary

this section briefly tells one of the Robin Hood stories

this paragraph summarises the legend

this paragraph gives the known facts about Robin Hood

in inverted commas because common names now, but open to debate over accuracy

4: 1: T27: to write a non-chronological report, including the use of organisational devices, e.g. numbered lists, headings for conciseness by:
● generalising some of the details
● deleting the least important details

Anansi

Background
This second extract from the *Oxford Children's Encyclopedia* is intended to describe and explain the various versions of Anansi, a character from many traditional tales and children's stories. The piece does not follow all the characteristics of the report genre, for example it is not written consistently in the present tense.

Shared reading and discussing the text
● Remind the children of any Anansi stories they have read, and re-read one if possible. See if the children can recall any other stories he is in. Explain that Anansi's main characteristic is that he tricks everyone he meets.
● Explain that the text is from an encyclopedia. It explains what the Anansi stories are about, where they come from and why they are popular.
● Read the extract through. Point out that although it includes a story, this is only an example, used to illustrate some of the factual information about Anansi stories. Explain that you can't ask *What happened next* of this sort of writing – it is called 'non-chronological' because it doesn't follow a time sequence.
● Ask the children to discuss what they have found out from the first two sentences. Explain that the opening of a report is usually a brief explanation of what is being described in more detail in the rest of the report. Would the children agree this is a good description? Point out how the rest of the paragraph describes Anansi and why he was so clever.
● Explain that in texts like this, each paragraph is about something new, and you can often give each paragraph a sub-heading. Split the class into four and give each group a paragraph to focus on. Can they come up with a sub-heading? Discuss whether the sub-heading really sums up what is said. You could also use the discussion to check understanding of what is written. Add effective sub-headings onto the text, using Post-it Notes.
● Point out the sub-heading that introduces the first of the 'sub-entries' ('Spider stories'). Is it a good one? Ask the children to review what

was included in the paragraph. Can they think of an alternative sub-heading? Ensure the children understand the storyteller's words.
● Explain that most reports are written in the present tense. They often start with statements like *Robins are birds*. Discuss what tense this text is in by highlighting the verbs in the first paragraph and identifying what it would say if it were written in the present tense. Then highlight the verbs in the fourth paragraph. Ask what tense they are. Discuss why there might be a change. (The first paragraph implies that Anansi is a figure from the past, confirmed by the second paragraph; the story is written, as most stories, in the past tense; it shifts to the present to talk about tricksters, suggesting that similar stories are still being told.)

Activities
● Give the children a grid with these column headings: *Paragraph [number]*, *Information included*, *Sub-heading*. Ask them to read each paragraph, identify the information included and decide upon a good sub-heading for it.
● Explain that many non-chronological reports include tables, pictures and diagrams to support reader's understanding. What diagrams or pictures might be useful with this extract? (Perhaps a map, an illustration of Anansi.) Ask the children to use the information provided to create accurate and supportive diagrams.
● Many reports end by relating the information to the reader. Ask a group to draft a new final paragraph that involves the reader, for example beginning *Perhaps you have a favourite Anansi story...* Talk about the use of direct appeal, questions and a friendly tone to communicate directly to a young reader. Discuss each sentence in turn with the group.

Extension/further reading
Ask a group to re-read the encyclopedia entry, then read an Anansi story. Does the character in the story fit with the figure described here?
Use an encyclopedia to find out more about the Asante people.

4: 1: T17: to identify features of non-fiction texts in print and IT, e.g. headings, lists, bullet points, captions which support the reader in gaining information efficiently

this type of text is intended to describe and explain something

Anansi's main characteristic

explanation of who and what Anansi was

each paragraph is about a different aspect of the Anansi stories

story within the information text

change of tense

Anansi

Anansi was a trickster god. He tricked everyone: other gods, human beings, animals, birds and insects. He could take any shape he liked, but he usually went about as a spider. That way, the creatures he was tricking never noticed him, or thought him harmless, until it was too late.

The Asante people of West Africa told the first stories about Anansi, and Africans who were taken as slaves to America and the Caribbean took the stories with them.

One of the best tells how the stories began. Anansi asked Nyankopon the sky-god to sell him a bag of stories, and the sky-god set what he thought was an impossible price: a hornet, a python, a leopard, a ghost and Anansi's own aged mother. But Anansi tricked his mother, a ghost, a leopard, a python and a nest of hornets into an old corn-sack and took them to Nyankopon. As soon as Nyankopon handed over the bag of stories, Anansi took them out one by one, changed the hero's name to Anansi and scattered them on the ground like seeds. However many Anansi stories people tell, hundreds more grow every day.

Stories about tricksters, like Anansi, are common in many countries. The trickster is a joker, a cunning fool and a prankster who does things that seem foolish but often turn out to be wise and clever. ■

Spider stories
Anansi means 'spider' in the Asante language. Among the Asante, it is said, these spider stories are only told at night, perhaps because they have power.
Before the story is told the teller may begin with something like:
"We do not really mean, we do not really mean that what we say is true."
And then the teller will end the story by saying something like:
"This, my spider story, which I have told, if it is sweet, if it is not sweet, take some somewhere else and let some come back to me."

English and Irish tricksters
Robin Goodfellow is the trickster of England. In Ireland he is to be found in the stories of Finn MacCool.

Other tricksters
The Winnebago Sioux, natives of North America, have a trickster called Hare. Brer Rabbit of the deep south of the USA is a trickster of a sort. In New Zealand, the Maoris have Mauii.

👁 **See also**
Brer Rabbit

sub-heading introduces a new element

the piece does not follow a time sequence

interesting detail about a related point

links to similar characters in other cultures

directs reader to a related entry elsewhere in the encyclopedia

4: 1: T27: to write a non-chronological report, including the use of organisational devices, e.g. numbered lists, headings for conciseness by:
● generalising some of the details
● deleting the least important details

A Hole in the Head

by Nicholas Fisk

Extract 1

Background

Science fiction stories often include clever inventions and gadgets like auto-heated clothes, but usually the most interesting aspect is when writers imagine that something fundamental about life as we know it has changed.

This extract is from a story set in the near future. Two children, Madi and Jonjo, live on OzBase, a research centre near the North Pole where their mother is examining the hole in the ozone layer. They are on the 'grey white wilderness' when they hear a dog barking.

Shared reading and discussing the text

● You may wish to read this text with a less able group prior to shared reading. If so, cover the last three sentences. Use the background notes as part of your introduction and clarify more challenging vocabulary. After independent reading, return to the text and discuss the setting and the characters' behaviour.

● Prior to reading with the whole class, as part of sentence-level work, you might want to revise children's understanding of apostrophes for contraction. Ask them to look out for them in the text, identifying the contraction and the full version. Prepare the text by covering the last three sentences.

● Explain the context of the extract and ask the children to be alert for any words, phrases or sentences that tell them about the setting, for example *Stay still, and your face aches and your fingers stiffen.* After reading, take suggestions and highlight the text. Identify the use of figurative language to illustrate the intensity of the cold: *The cold cuts right into you.*

● Explain that the story is set in the future; life is different from ours. Can the children identify anything that sounds like a new invention? (For example, *MetrePak* – probably a box or case, a metre cube, *auto-heated clothes.*)

● Focus now on the central event in this extract – the children hearing a dog bark. Remind the children of the context (the North Pole – an icy wilderness). Ask them to think why hearing a dog is extraordinary.

● Before re-reading, explain to the class that you want them to focus on how the children behave on hearing the dog; there are differences between the two. Look at the third paragraph. What does this tell us about Jonjo? Can they find any examples of him being cautious? (*Jonjo held her back.*)

● Now focus on Madi. Clarify the meaning of *reckless* and look for instances showing Madi's concern to get to the dog as quickly as possible, even though it's dangerous.

● Ask the children to discuss in pairs what they know about the dog. Model an answer: *One thing I know about the dog from the text is that it is trapped in a MetrePak.* What could they add? Encourage them to answer in an extended sentence and refer to the text.

● Can the children predict what the covered lines might say? Discuss possibilities, such as the dog biting the children. Then reveal the final sentences and re-read from *'Good dog,'* Madi said. What do they think of the ending? What do they notice about what the dog says? (It echoes what the children said to him.)

Activities

● Jonjo and Madi are both dressed well for the extreme conditions of the Artic. Ask children to make labelled diagrams identifying the special clothes that they are wearing.

● Ask a group to re-read the text, focusing on what they know and can infer about the dog. Encourage them to back up their ideas with reference to the text. For example, we know that the dog had been locked in a box from the evidence: *The MetrePak was open. And there was the dog.* We can infer that the dog is either very angry or very scared because it frantically lunges at the children.

Extension/further reading

Ask more able children to research the background to the hole in the ozone layer.

Grinny (Puffin Books) is another science fiction novel by Nicholas Fisk, particularly suitable for able readers.

4: 2: T1: to understand how writers create imaginary worlds, particularly where this is original or unfamiliar, such as a science fiction setting and to show how the writer has evoked it through detail

A Hole in the Head

Extract 1

And the dog kept (barking) barking, barking.

"We've got to do something!" Madi said. "Poor thing, it's tearing its throat to pieces!"

Jonjo stood still and said nothing. He was twelve, old enough to be cautious. Madi was two years younger, young enough to be reckless. She tugged at his arm.

"Please, Jonjo!" she said. "*Please!*"

Jonjo thought, Might as well do what she says. Can't just stand here. Stay still, and your face aches and your fingers stiffen. The cold cuts right into you…

"Come on!" she said, and trotted towards the MetrePak. She couldn't run properly, of course: not in all those layers of auto-heated clothes. He shambled after her. With each step, snow hissed and whispered beneath their boots.

They reached the MetrePak. A curved wedge of snow sealed the lid, but it was not locked. Jonjo pushed his thickly gloved fingers into the recessed handle and pulled. The lid came away. The MetrePak was open.

And there was the dog. Chained to a metal upright. It stopped barking – pulled at its chain, trying to reach them – and stood on its hind legs, scrabbling (desperately.)

"Good dog," Madi said, moving forward. "Nice dog."

Jonjo held her back. "Careful!" he said.

The dog (frantically) lunged at them. It twisted its head and gaped its mouth as if it were having a fit. Its collar strangled its throat. Its eyes rolled.

"Good boy," said Jonjo. He kept his voice low and steady. "What's your name, eh? Have you got a name?" (Very slowly,) he stretched out a hand protected by four thicknesses of fabric.

The dog seemed to have something stuck in its throat. It gasped, mouthed, swung its head. It gaped and showed sharp white teeth. Then, as if it were being sick, it brought up words.

The dog spoke.

"Good dog!" it said. "Good dog good!"

Annotations (left margin):
- establishes differences between the children
- metaphor – the cold is like a knife
- examples of how a science fiction writer can invent things which build up a sense of the future
- children's actions show their different characters
- a fearsome picture, dog appears wild and dangerous
- shows Jonjo taking care
- short, dramatic sentence

Annotations (right margin):
- this simple sound is extraordinary given the setting
- apostrophes for contraction suitable in speech
- Jonjo's thoughts highlight the harshness of the environment
- adverbs
- an unexpected climax, which takes reader by surprise

Annotation (bottom):
- this is the shocking change that has happened – scientists have been able to make dogs communicate in human languages

4: 2: T2: to understand how settings influence events and incidents in stories and how they affect characters' behaviour

4: 2: T4: to understand how the use of expressive and descriptive language can, e.g. create moods, arouse expectations, build tension, describe attitudes or emotions

4: 2: S2: to distinguish between uses of the apostrophe for contraction and possession

A Hole in the Head

by Nicholas Fisk

Extract 2

Background

This extract is from later in *A Hole in the Head*. Jonjo has been on a holiday to England with his mother while Madi stayed at the North Pole to look after the dog they had found. Madi has asked Jonjo to describe the changes that have occurred in England, since the climate had altered as a result of the hole in the ozone layer and global warming.

Shared reading and discussing the text

● Explain the context of this extract. If children have researched global warming their investigations would also be relevant as an introduction. In any case, explain that one of the predicted consequences of global warming is that sea levels will rise.

● Read the text to get a general overview of it. Point out that it is made up almost entirely of dialogue between the two children although nowhere does it say *said Madi*. Highlight the frequent use of apostrophes to mark contractions. Explain that it is a characteristic of speech to shorten words where possible. Can the children see any other aspects typical of spoken language? For example, childish 'slang': *marv*, exclamations: *Wow!*, italic used for emphasis, and 'incorrect', short sentences.

● To get a flavour of the conversation between the siblings, ask the children to act out in pairs the first four paragraphs. Tell them that Jonjo speaks first and encourage experimentation with the dialogue. Interrupt and ask them about how Jonjo and Madi are speaking. (Jonjo is excited, Madi wants him to focus on the details – she keeps interrupting.)

● Focus on the paragraphs that make up Jonjo's description of his visit. Read the one beginning *'They're producing wine.'* Can the children think of a title or sub-heading for this paragraph? (Perhaps *How England has changed*.) Do the same for the next three paragraphs.

● Focus on Jonjo's reaction to what he has seen, given in the last few paragraphs. Point out how his tone has changed, from excited to melancholic. Ask the children to explain why the sights were *sort of sad*. How would they have felt in the same situation?

● Return to the paragraph beginning *Everything was just as it was left* and explain that you want to write an additional paragraph after it, describing more of what Jonjo might have seen from his glass-bottomed boat. Model some opening sentences: *It looked really strange. You could see...*, then ask the children to offer contributions. Relate this more closely to their experience by asking them to imagine that it is their house underwater. What would they see if they were looking down on it? Complete the writing of the paragraph, drawing on a range of contributions.

Activities

● Give out cards of the central paragraphs of Jonjo's descriptions, each with the last sentence missing. Mount the missing sentences on separate cards. Ask the group to work out which sentence belongs with which paragraph. Encourage them to explain how they know. (They have to use context and meaning clues.)

● Some children could write an additional paragraph for the extract, to be added after *read the signs on the shops*. Remind them of the work you had done together and ask them to write their own version, perhaps using the same opening sentence(s).

● A group might design a poster to advertise trips by lectrilaunch to visit the sights of the deserted villages and towns of East Anglia. Remind the children of the importance of persuasive language and effective layout to make the poster sell the attractions.

Extension/further reading

Give children the opportunity to consider the similarities and differences between these extracts and those from *Woof!* and *Storm* (see pages 50–6).

The Weathermonger by Peter Dickinson (Puffin Books) imagines England to be under a spell that makes the people hate all machines. It is almost the opposite of a science fiction novel!

4: 2: T1: to understand how writers create imaginary worlds, particularly where this is original or unfamiliar, such as a science fiction setting and to show how the writer has evoked it through detail

4: 2: T2: to understand how settings influence events and incidents in stories and how they affect characters' behaviour

italic for emphasis

apostrophes are used frequently to mark contractions; used here in spoken language

A Hole in the Head

Extract 2

"Everything's changing so fast. Warming up. The seas getting warmer, swelling up and invading the land."

"Tell me *dramatic* things."

"All right, I'll tell you about the eastern bit of England. The sunken villages, they were dramatic. Wow!"

"Great, tell me."

"They're producing wine all over the southern half. It's got so warm that they've given up growing cereals and taken up wine grapes, bananas and mangoes and all that tropical stuff. Under plastic, of course, but all the same—"

"The *villages*."

"Oh, all right. You go to the east coast and hire glass-bottomed boats – there's fleets of them for the tourist trade. Great. And we had a boat to ourselves, Mum and I, a lectrilaunch called *Pandora*."

"Never mind the boat. Could you really see houses under the water?"

"You really could. Streets, roads, fences, the lot. It was weird. I mean, whole lumps of East Anglia are just swamped. They couldn't keep the sea out, the tides got higher and higher and the sea invaded, and all the people had to move inland."

"You could see houses and churches?"

"Everything was just as it was left. You could look down the chimneys of houses, even. See everything: old bikes that had been left behind, the old-style petrol cars they used before Dieselecs came in, even a motor coach. All rusting to nothing. In one place you could still read the signs on the shops."

"I wish I'd been there! It must have been *marv!*"

Jonjo did not reply at once. Then he said, "It wasn't really. It was sort of sad. But I couldn't stop looking."

"I'd have loved it!"

"I don't think so. After a time, you felt as if... as if you were spying... seeing things you're not supposed to see."

exclamations are another feature of speech

these paragraphs explain how England has changed because of global warming

slang and shorthand are features of speech, particularly children's

text does not tell who is speaking, but it is clear, as the long explanations are by Jonjo; this is the only speech tag

Madi is impatient for the details of the changes – she keeps questioning and interrupting

Jonjo is saddened by what has been lost

perhaps Jonjo feels like he is intruding on other people's lives or former lives

4: 2: T4: to understand how the use of expressive and descriptive language can, e.g. create moods, arouse expectations, build tension, describe attitudes or emotions

4: 2: T10: to develop use of settings in own writing, making use of work on adjectives and figurative language to describe settings effectively

4: 2: S2: to distinguish between uses of the apostrophe for contraction and possession

Beyond the Deepwoods by Paul Stewart

Background

This text is taken from the introduction to the first book in *The Edge Chronicles*, a series of fantasy stories by Paul Stewart and Chris Riddell. The stories are *tales that have been passed down the generations by word of mouth*.

Shared reading and discussing the text

● The text is challenging for less able readers. They might benefit from a guided reading session prior to whole class work. It is worth giving attention to the place names and other unfamiliar nouns as part of an introduction.

● Point out the opening three words and discuss how the reader is immediately placed in an imaginary world. (It suggests a fairy tale.) Next, highlight the simile *like the figurehead of a mighty stone ship* and discuss this image. (Something overhanging, reaching out into the emptiness.) Talk about the meaning of *edge* and that, in the past, people believed that there was an edge to the world, which you could fall off.

● Notice the rhythm as you read the second paragraph and point out the adjectival phrases *broad and swollen* and *large and loud*. What are they describing? (The river.) Can the children find other adjectives in the first sentence? (*Swirling* and *misty* describe the space beyond the Edge.) Notice how the verbs *roars* and *hurls* suggest the violence of the river. Alert the children to the importance of names.

● The third paragraph contrasts the river at its source with the wood in which it rises. Ask what the river is like at its source and identify the words that give the detail. Then ask about the Deepwoods. Highlight the important adjectives *dark* and *forbidding*.

● Paragraph 4 lists the creatures that live in the woods. Why is it surprising that so many live there? (Deepwoods is *forbidding, harsh* and *perilous*.) What do the children imagine them to be like? (The creatures' names are unpleasant; our knowledge of creatures from other fantasy stories raises certain expectations.)

● Paragraph 5 explains why people inhabit the Deepwoods. Point out how the horror and

danger is reinforced. What do the children think *sky pirates* and *Leagues-men* will be like?

● The last paragraph describes the Edgelands. Ask the children if they would like to go there. Given how awful all the places sound, what do they predict about the Twilight Woods? (They are *enchanting*, but *treacherous*.)

● Re-read the extract, then discuss it. Highlight how the author has created a setting, using place names and different characters, to intrigue the reader. His use of adjectives, careful verb choices and figurative language has created a vivid, frightening and strange setting. Ask the children to discuss what sort of story they would expect to follow this introduction.

Activities

● Use the information in the extract to draw a labelled map of the setting. Children who go on to read the rest of the book or other Edge Chronicles might complete the map using the rest of the introduction.

● A group might illustrate some of the shadowy creatures introduced in this extract. They could draw a picture and then describe the creature, using a range of interesting adjectives.

● Work with a group to re-read the text and list questions they have about the story. Use the questions in the plenary section, asking other children to answer them if possible.

● Help a group to agree details of their own imaginary world, developing a sketch map of their invented places in order to write an introduction. Identify a sequence, for example from the centre of the map to the outskirts or from the sea to the mountains, planning to use a paragraph to describe each area in turn. Scribe the first paragraph, challenging the children to provide detail and consider how best to express their ideas. Read the paragraph, then ask the children to work individually to create the rest of the introduction.

Extension/further reading

Compare this opening with the description of the Shire from *The Hobbit* by JRR Tolkein.

4: 2: T1: to understand how writers create imaginary worlds, particularly where this is original or unfamiliar… and to show how the writer has evoked it through detail

4: 2: T4: to understand how the use of expressive and descriptive language can, e.g. create moods, arouse expectations, build tension, describe attitudes or emotions

traditional, fairy tale opening; sets story in non-specific, perhaps magical, place

simile suggests a place reaching out into emptiness

perhaps the edge of the world

suggests non-stop motion of water

Beyond the Deepwoods

paragraph 1 sets the scene very effectively

Far far away, jutting out into the emptiness beyond, like the figurehead of a mighty stone ship, is the Edge. A torrent of water pours endlessly over the lip of rock at its overhanging point.

The river here is broad and swollen, and roars as it hurls itself down into the swirling, misty void below. It is difficult to believe that the river – like everything else that is large and loud and full of its own importance – might ever have been any different. Yet the origins of the Edgewater River could scarcely be humbler.

verbs suggest power and violence of river

adjectival phrases

paragraph 2 generates strong rhythm through punctuation and repetition

Its source lies far back inland, high up in the dark and forbidding Deepwoods. It is a small, bubbling pool, which spills over as a trickle and down along a bed of sandy gravel, little wider than a piece of rope. Its insignificance is multiplied a thousandfold by the grandeur of the Deepwoods themselves.

adjectives give an idea of what the Deepwoods are like

paragraph 3 presents a contrast to paragraph 2

Dark and deeply mysterious, the Deepwoods is a harsh and perilous place for those who call it home. And there are many who do. Woodtrolls, slaughterers, gyle goblins, termagant trogs: countless tribes and strange groupings scratch a living in the dappled sunlight and moonglow beneath its lofty canopy.

unpleasant names

It is a hard life and one fraught with many dangers – monstrous creatures, flesh-eating trees, marauding hordes of ferocious beasts, both large and small… Yet it can also be profitable, for the succulent fruits and buoyant woods which grow there are highly valued. Sky pirates and merchant Leagues-men vie for trade, and battle it out with one another high up above the endless ocean-green treetops.

paragraph 5 reinforces the sense of horror in the Deepwoods

Edgelands sound even worse than the Deepwoods!

Where the clouds descend, there lie the Edgelands, a barren wasteland of swirling mists, spirits and nightmares. Those who lose themselves in the Edgelands face one of two possible fates. The lucky ones will stumble blindly to the cliff edge and plunge to their deaths. The unlucky ones will find themselves in the Twilight Woods.

4: 2: T10: to develop the use of settings in own writing, making use of work on adjectives and figurative language to describe settings effectively

4: 2: S1: to revise and extend work on adjectives and link to work on expressive and figurative language in stories

4: 2: W9: to use alternative words and expressions which are more accurate or interesting than the common choices

Woof!

by Allan Ahlberg

Extract 1

Background

Fantasy fiction can take place in totally imaginary settings or involve supernatural events or other unreal happenings that are taken seriously. In this extract, Eric, a 'normal' boy, begins to turn into a dog for the first time.

Shared reading and discussing the text

● Read the first paragraph. Point out that although the sentences sound ordinary, they contain some extraordinary information. Ask what makes them sound ordinary. (The details of name and age, simple sentences that contain no adjectives or elaboration.) Before you read the next three paragraphs, explain that the author is establishing a very ordinary setting for his extraordinary story. Ask the children to notice the details of everyday life. Read the text, letting the children discuss what they notice. Prompt contributions: *What do we know about Eric? What had happened to Eric that day?*

● Remind the children that the idea that a boy could turn into a dog is extraordinary, fantastic. Ask why the author might want to set such a story in an ordinary house with an ordinary boy. (Setting amazing events in an everyday context makes the unusual events seem more believable, yet more amazing at the same time; unexpected events are funnier if they are set in a recognisable place and time.) Can the children think of any other stories that use this contrast between the ordinary and the amazing? (The Harry Potter stories, for example.)

● Focus on the second paragraph. Ask what sort of child Eric is. Then ask what sort of dog Eric would be. Eric could be just the same kind of character but in dog form, or completely different. Which would they think would be funnier? Scarier?

● Get the children to highlight where the phrase *a boy who turned into a dog* or similar is used. Ask why it is repeated. Explain that authors can raise expectations and interest by delaying or hinting at important events. Here we are told straight away what happens, but no details yet on how or why or the effects it had.

Alan Ahlberg never lets the reader forget what the story is about, even when giving a lot of detail about Eric's life.

● Read the final paragraph and ask how it begins to move the story on. Explain that not all of the paragraph is given here – what else would the author describe of Eric's change from boy to dog? What would happen to a person's hands, nose and ears for example?

Activities

● Use a cloze procedure with a group to focus on the language choices made to describe Eric's change. Remind the children that Ahlberg has tried to emphasise the ordinary and everyday setting of his story by using simple language. Ask the children to discuss their word choices. Which of the alternative versions do they prefer and why? With support, this is an appropriate activity for less able children.

● Re-read the text with a group. As a response to the text, ask the children to write three bullet points about either Eric or his family. Then tell them to sum up the information they have collected in a single sentence.

● Ask a group to complete the final paragraph. Remind them about the use of language in the piece. Set some constraints for their writing, for example they can only use four sentences and it must end *'I'm turning into a dog!'* After they have written one sentence, stop them to discuss how it sounds.

● Ask a group to rewrite one of the paragraphs in the extract so that instead of being very ordinary, Eric or his family seem larger than life. What would they change? Share their drafts during a plenary – how would such paragraphs change the meaning and effect of the extract?

Extension/further reading

Use a hot-seating activity to learn more about Eric and his family. Then help the children to write in role as Eric as he first changes into the dog. Remind them of the importance of sustaining the first person and making the text sound like Eric speaking.

4: 2: T1: to understand how writers create imaginary worlds, particularly where this is original or unfamiliar, and to show how the writer has evoked it through detail

this phrase is repeated a number of times

Woof!

Extract 1

1st paragraph (with simple sentences, no adjectives) presents an extraordinary idea as though it were quite normal and ordinary

There was once a boy who turned into a dog. The boy's name was Eric Banks; he was ten years old. The dog he turned into was a Norfolk terrier.

Eric Banks was a quiet boy, most of the time: 'steady worker', 'methodical', his school reports said. He was the kind of boy who didn't make a rush for the back seat of the bus, or go mad when the first snow fell. He was left-handed, right footed and rather small for his age. He had freckles.

these paragraphs contain lots of details about Eric, to build up a picture of his everyday life

Eric's life is carefully introduced to make it sound much like anyone else's

Eric lived with his parents and his little sister; her name was Emily, she was three. His dad was a postman; his mum had a part-time job in a shop. Eric himself had a paper-round which he shared with his friend, Roy Ackerman. (Actually, he was too young to have the round. It belonged to his cousin. But she had broken her arm, and Eric's dad was a friend of the newsagent… so, Eric was standing in.)

among all the detail of Eric's life, we are reminded of the extraordinary thing that is happening

Eric first turned into a dog a little at a time in his own bed. His parents were downstairs watching television. His sister was fast asleep in the next room. The time was ten past nine; the day, Wednesday; the month, June. Until then it had been a normal day for Eric. He'd done his paper-round with Roy, and gone to school. He'd had two helpings of his favourite dinner. He'd played with Emily before tea, and Roy after. He'd watched television, had a shower and gone to bed. Now he was *in* bed and turning into a dog.

the author is very precise about the time this happened, making the extraordinary seem more believable

It happened like this. Eric was lying on his side with his eyes closed. He was almost asleep. Suddenly, he felt an itch inside the collar of his pyjama jacket. This – although he didn't know it yet – was the fur sprouting.

it seems to be just a simple itch, but really something amazing is happening

4: 2: T2: to understand how settings influence events and incidents in stories and how they affect characters' behaviour

4: 2: T13: to write own examples of descriptive, expressive language based on those read. Link to work on adjectives and similes

Woof!

by Allan Ahlberg

Extract 2

P

131

Background

This is the second extract from *Woof!*, giving more detail of Eric's transformation.

Shared reading and discussing the text

● Remind the children of the previous extract from *Woof!* Explain that now we will learn more about Eric turning into a dog, then read the extract together.

● Highlight the sentence *His first action...* and the verb *scrabbling*. Explain that this verb describes Eric's dog-like actions. Can the children find similar examples from the first paragraph? (*Leapt, kicked, backed, growl.*) Ask why this is clever writing. (The language shows how Eric is becoming more dog-like.)

● Focus on the paragraph that describes Eric's room. What do the children make of the green light? Is it natural, given the green curtains, or is it suggesting some kind of magic?

● In the next two paragraphs, Eric thinks like a boy but acts increasingly like a dog. In pairs, ask the children to find examples of Eric's human thinking and dog behaviour. Do they think Eric is now more dog than human? Why might the author want Eric to go on thinking like a boy rather than a dog? (For one thing, it means that he can use Eric to comment on what has happened rather than having only a simple description of the changes.)

● Return to the first sentence. Highlight the simile *blurring and rippling like a swimmer under water.* Notice how this is effective because it makes a comparison that gives a vivid picture of the changes to Eric. Explain that you are going to write some other similes to express the changes. Say that you will write as Eric, so will use the first person pronoun, *I*. Start with: *I was turning into a dog.* Explain that you will now use a simile to bring the writing to life: *My body melted like snow off a roof in the weak wintry sun.* Discuss whether the simile works. How could it be improved?

● List other verbs that could be used in similes to express the transformation into a dog, for example *shivered, shuddered, twitched,* coughed, barked. Can the children suggest other verbs? Ask them to work in pairs to use the verbs in new similes, using the same introduction as before. List ideas and discuss which make good comparisons and express effectively what has happened.

Activities

● Support the writing of a paragraph that describes the change in Eric from boy to dog by providing a writing frame. The frame should encourage the use of similes, for example: *I was turning into a dog. My body... like... My hands... My face... My ears... My feet... I was like a...* Talk about the kinds of language that would fit. Encourage the children to use powerful verbs to create interesting similes.

● More independent groups could do the same activity without the supporting frame. Provide the first line and ask them to create their own paragraph. When they have produced a draft, begin a guided writing session focused on improving and extending their ideas. Share the different adjectives and similes used and discuss why some are particularly effective. Allow the children to improve their paragraphs in the light of the discussion.

● Decide with a group the features of a particular animal – claws, teeth and so on – and list them. Then ask the children to think of an adjective to describe one of the features: *sharp claws.* Demonstrate how to make this more interesting by adding a simile: *sharp claws like tiny daggers ripping at my clothes.* Ask them to write a list of an animal's features and think of some strong adjectives to describe them to work on creating interesting comparisons beginning with the word *like*.

● In the last paragraph there are rhetorical questions. Ask children to explain briefly why they think Eric has changed into a dog.

Extension/further reading

Read other examples of stories of humans being transformed into animals, for example Philip Pullman's *I Was a Rat!* (Corgi).

4: 2: T2: to understand how settings influence events and incidents in stories and how they affect characters' behaviour

4: 2: T4: to understand how the use of expressive and descriptive language can, e.g. create moods, arouse expectations, build tension, describe attitudes or emotions

4: 2: T5: to understand the use of figurative language in poetry and prose; compare poetic phrasing with narrative/descriptive examples; locate use of simile

Woof!

Extract 2

very precise timings given; detail adds to creation of believable image for the reader

very effective simile to portray the transformation

The time it took Eric to turn into a dog – his shape blurring and rippling like a swimmer under water – was about fifteen seconds. The time it took him to become frantic was about five seconds after that. His first action was to begin scrabbling in the bed, trying to get a better look at himself. His thoughts were in turmoil: "I'm a dog! A *dog*!" The next thing he did was try to get out of bed. This wasn't easy for a dog in pyjamas; besides, they were baggy on him now. Eric leapt, and landed in a heap. He kicked his way clear of the trousers and backed out of the jacket. He resisted the urge to growl when one of his claws got caught in a buttonhole. He sat on the floor and thought: "I'm a dog!"

verb choices suggest that Eric is starting to act and behave like a dog

humour

It was now a quarter past nine. The last of the evening sunlight was shining through the green curtains. Everything in the room – furniture and wallpaper, Eric's books and toys, his junior science kit, his clothes laid out on a chair beside the bed – was tinged with green light. Birds were chirruping outside the window. Next door, Mr Phipps was mowing his lawn.

everything looks strange, suggesting that something magical is happening

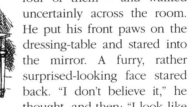

Eric got to his feet – all four of them – and walked uncertainly across the room. He put his front paws on the dressing-table and stared into the mirror. A furry, rather surprised-looking face stared back. "I don't believe it," he thought, and then: "I look like a Norfolk terrier." Eric knew a bit about dogs. He'd done a project on them with Roy in the second year.

Eric's physical features and movements are those of a dog, but he still thinks like a person – he can comment, from the inside, about this extraordinary event!

Once more Eric sat on the floor. He was bewildered, to say the least. A confusion of questions jostled in his head: "How could it happen? What's the cause of it? Why me?" He went to the window, put his paws on the sill, ducked his head under the curtain and looked out.

Eric's reactions are very understandable!

4: 2: T13: to write own examples of descriptive, expressive language based on those read. Link to work on adjectives and similes

4: 2: S1: to revise and extend work from Year 3 term 2 on adjectives and link to work on expressive and figurative language in stories

Storm

by Kevin Crossley-Holland

Extract 1

Background

This text is from the beginning of a short ghost/ mystery novel. Like many fantasy adventures (of which ghost stories could be considered a sub-genre), in this tale, a child encounters a magical, rather frightening force. This extract builds up an eerie atmosphere through description and reference to strange events or creatures.

Shared reading and discussing the text

● Consider the title of the extract. What does it suggest? (Bad weather, something frightening, bad temper, a name?) Use the discussion to raise expectations of the text.

● Read the first paragraph and point out the name of the town. Explain how this could be read two ways (*Waters lain* – lying water or *Water slain* – killed by water). What is the author suggesting? Why?

● Help the children to identify other 'sinister' elements in this paragraph, such as the effect of repeated *s* sounds. Highlight the sentence: *Empty it looked and silent it seemed.* Ask the children to discuss the meaning and any inference. Point out the balance in the sentence, which gives it a satisfying tone and rhythm.

● Ask if Annie is scared by the lonely marsh. Ask pairs of children to find evidence that she loves it. (For example, *but Annie knew better.*) Read the second paragraph and see if they can they find more evidence. Identify the alliteration of *b* sounds – a more comforting, rounded, soft sound than the *s* of the first paragraph.

● Before you read paragraph 3, explain that the marsh is different in winter. Ask the children to identify one or two things that Annie does not like. Point out the effective use of adjectives (*steely, horrible*) and powerful verbs (*screamed*) that convey some of Annie's fear. Check understanding of unusual words like *boggarts*.

● Explain that one of the most frightening stories in the neighbourhood is about a horseman. Set the children up to notice the ghost, what it was supposed to do and the impact that the stories have on Annie. Then read paragraph 4 and discuss what they notice.

Pick out what the last line implies: that she was afraid of the ford in the dark.

● Re-read the whole extract. Stop after each paragraph and ask the children what they know for sure (what is literally stated) and what they think it might mean (their inference). Encourage the children to predict what might happen.

Activities

● Focus on the characterisation of Annie by dramatising her walks along the track in summer and in winter. Ask individuals to bring the walk to life, like a short video extract. The rest of the class should check whether the actor has conveyed Annie's mood correctly. Focus on her actions in the story and decide whether they show that she is happy or frightened.

● Begin an alphabet alliteration activity, to be completed over a number of days, where children suggest an alliterative phrase to describe the actions of an animal or natural phenomenon. You could take examples from the text, such as *seabirds scream, wind whines*.

● The extract describes a number of mysterious, frightening events and characters. Ask a group to write in role as someone who finds the stories silly. How would they explain strange events like the dropping of the shopping?

● Ask a less able group to focus on the last paragraph and to underline in different colours two things that the ghost had done at the ford. Then talk about the meaning of the second sentence of the paragraph. Are the ghost's actions just tricks or something worse?

Extension/further reading

Storm is a short novel, very suitable for children beginning to read independently. They could keep a reading journal as they read it, noting what has happened and predicting what they thought would happen next. Encourage them to check their predictions as they progress through the book.

Paul Theroux's *A Christmas Card* (Puffin Books) also involves a mysterious, perhaps ghostly, stranger changing the life of a family.

4: 2: T1: to understand how writers create imaginary worlds, particularly where this is original or unfamiliar and to show how the writer has evoked it through detail

4: 2: T2: to understand how settings influence events and incidents in stories and how they affect characters' behaviour

precise setting – contributes to reader's appreciation of Annie's isolation

effective balance and rhythm

alliteration introduces sinister element

alliteration of soft 'b' sounds is more friendly; Annie clearly loves playing around the marsh in summer

harsh alliteration

stories about ghost could be explained in other ways, but Annie believes them and is frightened

STORM

Extract 1

Their cottage stood on its own at the edge of the great marsh, two miles away from the village of Waterslain. That marsh! Empty it looked and silent it seemed, but Annie knew better. She knew about the nests among the flags and rushes, she knew where to find the dark pools teeming with shrimps and scooters. She knew the calls of the seabirds, the sucking sound of draining mud, the wind hissing in the sea lavender.

Everyday in termtime Annie had to walk along this track at the edge of the marsh. She had to take off her shoes and socks to paddle across the ford of the river Rush, the little stream that bumbled all summer, but burbled and bustled all winter when it was sometimes as much as twenty paces across. And then she hurried up the pot-holed lane to the crossroads where the school bus picked her up at twenty to nine and took her into Waterslain.

The only thing that Annie didn't like were the steely winter days when it began to grow dark before she came home from school. The marsh didn't seem such a friendly place then. The wind whined, seabirds screamed. At night, the boggarts and bogles and other marsh spirits showed their horrible faces. Once, Annie had heard the Shuck, the monster dog, coming up behind her and had only just got indoors in time.

Worst of all was the ghost who haunted the ford. Annie's mother said that he didn't mean to harm anyone, he just liked to play tricks on them and scare them. On one occasion Mrs Carter had dropped a basket of shopping into the water, and she complained that the ghost had given her a push from behind. And the farmer, Mr Elkins, told Annie he had heard shouting and whinnying at the ford, but could see no man or horse to go with them. Annie always ran down the lane after school in winter so that she could get past the ford before it was completely dark.

name can be read in 2 ways – 'waters lain' or 'water slain' – adds to the mystery

effective adjective grey, hard and cold

adjectives and verbs create a picture of a frightening place – marsh seems to be filled with sinister creatures, or so the stories would suggest

are these real? has Annie been told stories about them or are they just her imagination? had she really heard something?

implies that she is frightened, so wants to get away from the ford, to avoid encountering the ghost

4: 2: T4: to understand how the use of expressive and descriptive language can, e.g. create moods, arouse expectations, build tension, describe attitudes or emotions

4: 2: S1: to revise and extend work on adjectives from Year 3 term 2 and link to work on expressive and figurative language in stories

4: 2: W1: to read words through grammatical and contextual knowledge when reading unfamiliar texts

Storm

by Kevin Crossley-Holland

Extract 2

Background

Annie is about to walk across the marsh to the village of Waterslain, two miles away, in the middle of the night and during a terrible storm. She has to go because the storm has brought the telephone lines down and her sister is about to have her baby. Annie is going to fetch a doctor. As she is about to leave, the family hears the sound of a horse approaching.

Shared reading and discussing the text

● Explain the context of this extract and then read the passage with the children. Ensure comprehension of the events.
● Ask the children to talk in pairs to suggest adjectives that describe the horseman (such as *strange*, *mysterious*). Ask them why they would describe the horseman in this way.
● Focus on the conversation between Mr Carter and the horseman, from *The horseman stopped…* Ask them to decide what each character might be thinking at this point.
● Now ask two children to act or read out the conversation. What do they learn about the horseman from the conversation? (Very little!)
● Return to the text. Highlight all the information about the horseman. Can the children identify the ways that the author has made the horseman seem mysterious? (For example, the time of night, riding in a storm, his appearance, his *dark voice*, his lack of name.) You might remind the children of the previous extract. Was there any clue in that about this strange figure?
● Tell the class that you think Annie is frightened here. Ask them to find evidence to support this judgement. Reinforce how the author captures Annie's fears through her actions (*slipped one hand inside her mother's hand*), her reluctance (evident in what she says to her mother and the horseman), and through the adverb in *Annie's heart was beating fearfully.*
● Look closely at the last sentence of the extract to explore the use of language. Focus on the verb *swallowed* and the adjective *stormy.* Why are they effective choices? What

do they suggest? (They reinforce the setting, add to the mystery and convey Annie's fear.) Ask the class to find and discuss other examples of powerful verb choices in the passage.
● Point out two other ominous phrases – *said not a word* and *if there was a need*. Both are quite unusual; they sound old fashioned.

Activities

● Children could write the next paragraph to continue the story, describing the first part of Annie's journey across the marsh. Remind them what they know about the horseman, Annie and the setting. Recap how the author conveys feelings and the sense of mystery through his careful choice of words.
● Ask a group of three to create a frozen picture of Annie and the horseman's ride and then bring it to life. Two of the group should be the characters, the third should be the stage director, giving them ideas about how they should stand, look and what they might say. Swap roles so each child has a turn at each role. With support for less able writers, this might lead into writing a dialogue between the characters.
● Explore the figurative language of *as light as thistledown*. Can the children create a list of alternative similes that begin *as light as*? In the plenary, talk about how their images are different from the original.
● Ask a group to highlight all of the adjectives used in the passage. Although there are not many, they are important in establishing the mood of the story. Against each one, ask the group to explain what it suggests about its subject. For example, Annie's face is described in a metaphor as *the full white moon*. Does this suggest she is pale with fright?

Extension/further reading

Read the two extracts again and ask for predictions on who the horseman is and what might happen as the story unfolds. If possible, allow children to read the complete story to confirm their predictions.

4: 2: T2: to understand how settings influence events and incidents in stories and poems and how they effect characters' behaviour

4: 2: T4: to understand how the use of expressive and descriptive language can, e.g. create moods, arouse expectations, build tension, describe attitudes or emotions

STORM

Extract 2

Annie slipped one hand inside her mother's hand. The hooves drummed louder and louder, almost on top of them, and round the corner of the cottage galloped a horseman on a fine chestnut mare.

"Whoa!" shouted the rider when he saw Annie and her family standing at the cottage door.

"That's not Elkins, then," said Mr Carter, hauling himself in front of his wife and daughters. "That's not his horse."

The horseman stopped just outside the pool of light streaming through the open door, and none of them recognised him. He was tall and unsmiling.

"That's a rough old night," Mr Carter called out.

The horseman nodded and said not a word.

"Are you going into Waterslain?"

"Waterslain?" said the horseman. "Not in particular."

"Blast!" said Mr Carter in a thoughtful kind of way.

"I could go," said the horseman in a dark voice, "if there was a need."

Then Annie's mother loosed her daughter's hand and stepped out into the storm and soon explained the need, and Mr Carter went out and asked the horseman his name. The wind gave a shriek and Annie was unable to catch his reply. "So you see," said Annie's mother, "there's no time to be lost."

"Come on up, Annie," said the horseman.

"It's all right," said Annie, shaking her head.

"I'll take you," said the horseman.

"You'll be fine," said Mrs Carter.

"I can walk," insisted Annie.

But the horseman quickly bent down and put a hand under one of Annie's shoulders and swung her up on to the saddle in front of him as if she were as light as thistledown.

Annie's heart was beating fearfully. She bit hard on her lower lip.

Then the horseman raised one hand and spurred his horse. Mr and Mrs Carter stood and watched as Annie turned away the full white moon of her face and then she and the horseman were swallowed in the stormy darkness.

---

a sign that Annie needs reassurance; she is frightened

threatening, frightening

horseman does not seem friendly

the need (reason) is that Willa, Annie's sister, is about to give birth

Annie does not want to go with the horseman

this paragraph clearly states Annie's fear; putting these two short sentences on their own emphasises this

description suggests she is pale and scared; reinforces the darkness of the night

indicates difficulty and effort; Mr Carter cannot walk or move easily

horseman seems to be avoiding the light or positioning himself so he cannot easily be seen

lack of conversation adds to the mystery of the horseman

interesting choice of adjective

horseman's name remains a mystery

simile – Annie is either very light or the horseman is very strong (or does not notice weight)

metaphor – the darkness 'ate' them

4: 2: T13: to write own examples of descriptive, expressive language based on those read. Link to work on adjectives and similes

4: 2: S1: to revise and extend work on adjectives from Year 3 term 2 and link to work on expressive and figurative language in stories

4: 2: W9: to use alternative words and expressions which are more accurate or interesting than the common choices

Granny Granny Please Comb My Hair

by Grace Nichols

134

Background

Grace Nichols is a Caribbean-British poet. Her poems often explore ordinary events and relationships in language strongly influenced by her background. The following two poems have a similar focus on family and everyday life and use children as their speakers; they sometimes use dialectal forms and vocabulary.

Shared reading and discussing the text

● Enjoy the poem with the class and talk about the theme. What sort of person is the speaker's Granny? Identify the simile *parting gentle as a breeze* and explain how this gives a clear idea of how careful Granny is. Relate the theme to the children's own experiences. Do their grandparents have more time for them than their parents? Does anyone else? Then ask whether the title of the poem is a good one. Get them to explain why.

● Ask about the speaker of the poem. What sort of person, what sort of age do they imagine her to be? (There is no right answer, but the reader can infer information.) After paired discussion, take ideas from different groups and ask them to justify their answers.

● Re-read the poem. Notice that it sounds like a person talking. Can the children see how this is achieved? (By the use of repetition and by directly addressing Granny.) Encourage children to highlight examples of repetition of words and phrases. Suggest they also look out for lines including the pronoun *you*.

● Look at the rhyme scheme of the poem. Re-read the first verse and identify the rhyme of *hair* and *care*. Discuss the different spelling patterns that represent the same phoneme. Do a similar exercise with the rhyme in verse 2. Alert them to verse 3, where there is not a full rhyme, but two half or near rhymes (of *mummy* and *hurry*, and *rush* and *tugs*). Finally, in the last verse, establish that there isn't a rhyme. Although *Granny* and *say* end with the same letter, the word endings do not have the same phonemes. Conclude by asking the class to suggest why the poet didn't maintain a regular

rhyme scheme. (Perhaps to add to the change from the regular rhythm of Granny's brushing to the rush of Mummy in a hurry.)

Activities

● Groups might use the poem as a model for their own writing. Ask them to choose a special person to be the subject. The first line of their poem would be the person's name. Ask the group to think of three or four 'pictures' of this person and plan the poem by making brief notes or sketches. Remind them of how Grace Nichols makes her poem sound like speech. After the first verse, check that the children are achieving the right tone. Ask them to discuss what they are going to write next. You might stop less confident writers after each verse. Finally, ask them to give their poem a title.

● Ask a group to prepare a reading of Grace Nichols' poem, interpreting the words as if they were an actor's script, perhaps trying different tones of voice to suggest certain attitudes. They could tape their different versions to improve them later or appoint a 'director' to make constructive comments. This could be developed into an acting performance by introducing actions and dialogue into the text. This might be presented to other groups who could offer comments.

● Demonstrate how each verse, although about the same subject, presents a different picture of family life. In groups, get children to pose in a 'photograph' of the characters in verses 2, 3 and 4. Encourage them to justify their positions by referring to the text. You could extend the work by asking the 'actors' to express the character's thoughts. (For example, in verse 3, Mummy might be thinking about having to rush off to work.)

Extension/further reading

Create an anthology of poems by Grace Nichols, such as 'Morning' in *Read Me: A Poem A Day for the National Year of Reading* (Macmillan). Encourage children to consider how many of them describe scenes from everyday life.

50 Shared texts ● Year 4

4: 2: T4: to understand how the use of expressive and descriptive language can, e.g. create moods, describe attitudes or emotions

4: 2: T5: to understand the use of figurative language in poetry and prose; compare poetic phrasing with narrative/ descriptive examples; locate use of simile

uses the way children speak

everyday subject

it is the time and care that Granny gives that makes this ordinary experience special

Mummy's hair-brushing contrasts with Granny's; she doesn't mean to hurt, but doesn't take as much care

repetition and very short line emphasise speed and lack of care

repeats an idea from 1st verse

Granny seems to take as much pleasure from this as her granddaughter

Granny Granny
Please Comb My Hair

Granny Granny
please comb my hair
you always take your time
you always take such care

You put me to sit on a cushion
between your knees
you rub a little coconut oil
parting gentle as a breeze

Mummy Mummy
She's always in a hurry-hurry
rush
she pulls my hair
sometimes she tugs

But Granny
you have all the time in the world
and when you're finished
you always turn my head and say
"Now who's a nice girl."

Grace Nichols

this rhyming pattern recurs in verse 2

simile – gives a clear picture of the care and gentleness with which Granny treats her granddaughter, and conveys the pleasant feeling

half-rhymes in verse 3

no rhyme at all in last verse

4: 2: T7: to identify different patterns of rhyme and verse in poetry, and to read these aloud effectively

4: 2: T11: to write poetry based on the structure and/or style of poems read, e.g. taking account of vocabulary, patterns of rhyme, similes

4: 2: W1: to read words through
● identifying phonemes in speech and writing
● blending phonemes for reading
● segmenting words into phonemes

The Older the Violin the Sweeter the Tune

by John Agard

P

Background
This poem is by a West Indian poet living in the UK. It has similarities in terms of subject and style with 'Granny Granny Please Comb My Hair', although it is more challenging in terms of its language, which is strongly dialectal.

Shared reading and discussing the text
● Explain that John Agard often writes in a form of West Indian English and some words may be unfamiliar, particularly as written rather than simply spoken words. For example, clarify *me* ('my') and *dih* and *de* (both 'the'). Read the poem a number of times and check understanding.
● Point out that the title is also used in the third verse, this time in dialect and with speech marks. Can the children explain why? (It is Granny's direct speech.) Let the children discuss what the phrase means, then explain that it is a metaphor – Granny is comparing herself to an old violin, which sounds better than a new one.
● Tell the children that similes are used to make two other comparisons. Ask them to find the simile in the first verse (*stories shine like a moon*) and ask them to discuss what it means. (Granny's stories are full of life and brightness.) Then identify *Me Granny must be wiser / than the man inside the moon* as another simile. Ask children in pairs to explain the meaning. Take ideas. Ensure understanding; the simile is comparing Granny to the man in the moon, suggesting she is even wiser than he is supposed to be!
● Focus now on the pattern of verses and the rhyme. Point out the differences in verse length. Ask the children to identify the rhymes in verses 1 and 2. Re-read the final five lines and ask about the rhyme there. Examine the different spelling patterns of the rhyming phoneme.
● Remind the children of 'Granny Granny Please Comb My Hair' and work with them to list some of the obvious similarities and differences. Explain which of the two you prefer, modelling how to back up an opinion

with reasons. (For example, *I prefer 'Granny Granny…' because I like the pictures of ordinary life it gives.*) Children should discuss in pairs their own favourite, giving reasons.

Activities
● 'The Older the Violin the Sweeter the Tune' uses language exuberantly. Ask children to try to capture this on a taped reading of the poem.
● Ask a group to develop a series of questions for John Agard, about the poem and the way he writes. In a plenary, take the role of the poet and answer the questions drafted.
● Explain that you want to write a poem using 'The Older the Violin…' as a model. Decide on a subject, such as 'My Dad', and demonstrate how to begin, for example *Me daddy cool / Me daddy fine*. Break there and remind the group of the use of similes and non-standard forms like *me* and *de*. Suggest a simile to complete the first verse of your poem, for example *Me daddy is as smooth / As a carefully drawn line.* Encourage children to invent their own similes, if possible making them rhyme. Include one in your draft and move on to the next verse.
● Mention that in Agard's poem this second verse shows things that Granny could and couldn't do. *What about our poem?* Encourage the children to draft the next three lines, working in pairs. On completion, ask them to re-read the lines, checking whether they rhyme. Prepare them to write the last five lines independently by looking at how the original works – verse 3 introduces a saying, verse 4 sum up Granny. Ask children to have a go at using this model.

Extension/further reading
Ask an able group to make a comparison chart of the features of 'The Older the Violin…' and 'Granny Granny…'. They could list features, such as non-standard English and rhyme, in the left-hand column and tick or cross to say whether the features are to be found in each of the poems.

4: 2: T4: to understand how the use of expressive and descriptive language can, e.g. create moods, arouse expectations, build tension, describe attitudes or emotions

4: 2: T5: to understand the use of figurative language in poetry; locate use of simile

4: 2: T7: to identify different patterns of rhyme and verse in poetry, e.g. rhyming couplets, alternate line rhymes, and to read these aloud effectively

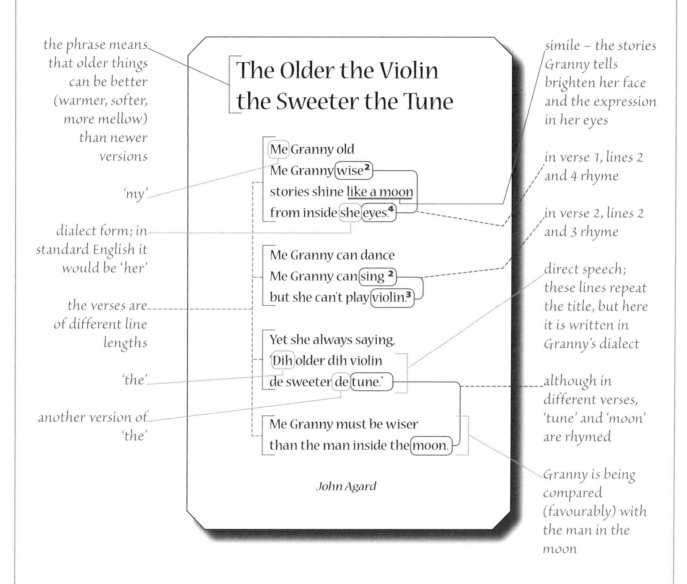

the phrase means that older things can be better (warmer, softer, more mellow) than newer versions

'my'

dialect form; in standard English it would be 'her'

the verses are of different line lengths

'the'

another version of 'the'

The Older the Violin the Sweeter the Tune

Me Granny old
Me Granny wise²
stories shine like a moon
from inside she eyes.⁴

Me Granny can dance
Me Granny can sing ²
but she can't play violin.³

Yet she always saying,
"Dih older dih violin
de sweeter de tune."

Me Granny must be wiser
than the man inside the moon.

John Agard

simile – the stories Granny tells brighten her face and the expression in her eyes

in verse 1, lines 2 and 4 rhyme

in verse 2, lines 2 and 3 rhyme

direct speech; these lines repeat the title, but here it is written in Granny's dialect

although in different verses, 'tune' and 'moon' are rhymed

Granny is being compared (favourably) with the man in the moon

4: 2: T11: to write poetry based on the structure and/or style of poems read, e.g. taking account of vocabulary, archaic expressions, patterns of rhyme, similes

4: 2: W1: to read words through using phonic knowledge as a cue, together with grammatical and contextual knowledge, when reading unfamiliar texts

Honey I Love by Eloise Greenfield

Background

Eloise Greenfield is an African-American poet. This poem springs from a similar cultural background to the previous two poems and there are similarities in terms of subject.

Shared reading and discussing the text

● Recap that the other poems read in this unit use rhyme and repetition to make words sound like someone speaking. Ask the children to listen out for the same effects in this poem.

● Read this poem once and ask the children if they have noticed any rhyme and repetition. The scheme in the main part is very regular (AABB) and the last line of each verse repeats some of the line before. The penultimate line of most verses is also similar, using the refrain of *Honey, let me tell you.*

● Explain that the repetition acts a bit like a chorus, holding the poem together. Highlight the opening three and closing four lines of the poem and point out the near repetition. These lines also help to organise the poem.

● Ask the children to re-read the poem then tell you what they think it is about. Clarify the reference to *flying pool* in verse 2 (the hose makes a pool of water, the children make the water 'fly' by jumping in).

● Re-read up to verse 5 and explain that the next verse is different. Ask the class to hear how the pattern is broken. The fourth line emphasises a negative and the first line uses *but* rather than *and* to join two ideas.

● Identify that the poem is a series of descriptions of things that the speaker likes. It is similar to 'Granny Granny...' in that it could be illustrated with photographs.

● Demonstrate how to write in the style of this poem. Write the same opening lines, then stop briefly to talk about something that you love doing, noting some of the details on the board. Remind the class how 'Honey I Love' presents 'pictures', and that very few adjectives are used. Also explain that the lines are quite long – either one idea is expanded or two shorter ideas are linked. Draft two or three lines, using your

notes and explaining word choices you make. Repeat part of the penultimate line as the last line. For example:

I love
I love a lot of things, a whole lot of things
Like
When my friends come to visit and they bring a guitar along
'Cause they play such sweet music and they sing such sweet songs
I like the way they gabble and all the jokes they say
Honey, let me tell you that I LOVE the way they play
    I love the way they play
        and

Revise the draft. Don't worry if your version does not rhyme. You should find that by repeating lines the poem should sound quite effective. Talk about differences between your poem and the original.

Activities

● Ask a group to improve the ideas you drafted together, perhaps exploring how to make the lines rhyme and make better word choices.

● With a less able group, repeat the shared writing activity, using their own ideas as the basis for drafting and reshaping the verses. Use the original poem's introductory and closing lines as a means of structuring the writing.

● Encourage more able children to manipulate the pattern to express their own ideas. Stop them after one verse to re-read their draft, check for sense and their use of the structure and rhyme scheme of the original. Explain that sense is more important than rhyme; a poem with a clear structure will sound effective.

Extension/further reading

Continuing work on the comparison chart from page 60 would make for a useful discussion of similarities and differences between the three poems, including subject and voice.

4: 2: T4: to understand how the use of expressive and descriptive language can, e.g. create moods, arouse expectations, build tension, describe attitudes or emotions

4: 2: T7: to identify different patterns of rhyme and verse in poetry, e.g. choruses, rhyming couplets, alternate line rhymes and to read these aloud effectively

these lines act as a kind of introduction to the poem

capitals to suggest how the word should be said – with emphasis

Honey I Love

I love
I love a lot of things, a whole lot of things
Like
My cousin comes to visit and you know he's from the South
'Cause every word he says just kind of slides out of his mouth
I like the way he whistles and I like the way he walks
But honey, let me tell you that I LOVE the way he talks
I love the way my cousin talks
and

The day is hot and icky and the sun sticks to my skin A
Mr Davis turns the hose on, everybody jumps right in A
The water stings my stomach and I feel so nice and cool B
Honey let me tell you that I LOVE a flying pool B
I love to feel a flying pool
and

Renee comes out to play and brings her doll without a dress
I make a dress with paper and that doll sure looks a mess
We laugh so loud and long and hard the doll falls to the ground
Honey, let me tell you that I LOVE the laughing sound
I love to make the laughing sound
and

My uncle's car is crowded and there's a lot of food to eat
We're going down the country where the church folks like to meet
I'm looking out the window at the cows and trees outside
Honey, let me tell you that I LOVE to take a ride
I just love to take a family ride
and

My mama's on the sofa sewing buttons on my coat
I go and sit beside her, I'm through playing with my boat
I hold her arm and kiss it, 'cause it feels so soft and warm
Honey, let me tell you that I LOVE my mama's arm
I love to kiss my mama's arm
and

It's not so late at night, but still I'm lying in my bed
I guess I need my rest, at least that's what my mama said
She told me not to cry 'cause she don't want to hear a peep
Honey, let me tell you I DON'T love to go to sleep
I do not love to go to sleep

But I love
I love a lot of things, a whole lot of things
And honey,
I love you, too.

Eloise Greenfield

the pattern of the last line in each verse is sustained throughout the poem

the verses are like snapshots of different events; they act as a kind of list

this verse stands out by describing what the speaker does not like

the last verse is like a condensed version of the 1st

very regular rhyme scheme maintained throughout

compare this 'negative' connective with the others used

emphasis on the negative

4: 2: T11: to write poetry based on the structure and/or style of poems read, e.g. taking account of vocabulary, patterns of rhyme, similes

4: 2: W9: to use alternative words and expressions which are more accurate or interesting than the common choices

4: 2: S4: to recognise how commas, connectives and full stops are used to join and separate clauses

Windy Nights by Robert Louis Stevenson

Background

'Classic' poems are those which many readers love even though they may have been written some time ago and their subject matter might be out of date or unfamiliar. Stevenson's collection *A Child's Garden of Verses*, from which this poem comes, has been in print ever since it was first published in 1885.

Shared reading and discussing the text

● Prepare the text by covering some of the rhyming words in the second verse. You might want to cover up the second verse too at first.

● Read the first verse. What do the children think is happening? Ask about the setting, such as the time of day, and the horseman.

● Help the children to realise how much they know about the setting in comparison with about the rider. Help them to understand that by telling them little, the poet creates a mystery. Point out how the verse ends with a question, and ask what else they would like to know.

● Explore some style features of the first verse. Point out the rhyme scheme. Making the final two lines rhyme gives a sense of completeness to the verse, it sounds 'finished'. Also point out the repetition (of *whenever, night* and *gallop*) and the use of *i*-sound assonance. The poem is creating a sense of mystery, rather than describing events. The poem also has a strong sense of rhythm or beat. Get the children to beat out, for example with their fingers or a drum, the points of emphasis in some of the lines. Discuss how the repetition of words also contributes to this rhythm.

● Introduce the second verse with the rhymes covered. In pairs, ask the children to suggest what would rhyme, reminding them of the rhyme scheme. Discuss which ideas fit best.

● Ask if the second verse includes any examples of repetition (*by, goes, gallop*) or assonance (*low, goes*). Discuss why there is so much repetition – perhaps to suggest the horseman continually riding back and forwards.

● Return to setting and character. What have we learned about the setting from verse 2?

(Very little that is new, but the images of stormy weather are reinforced.)

● Focus on the rider. Help the children to see, perhaps by asking unanswerable questions such as *What does the rider look like?*, that they are told almost nothing about him, but they can still imagine him. Consider explanations for the rider's behaviour. Perhaps he is a ghost, a highwayman, he is looking for someone.

Activities

● Ask a group to plan a series of four drawings to illustrate the poem. What would be included in each drawing? How would they convey the mysterious nature of the rider? (For example, by not showing his face.)

● Rework the first verse with a group. Retain the second and third lines but draft new first and third lines, for example:

Whenever the rain is bruising the leaves
Whenever the wind…
And the shadow of the fox blends into the trees
A man…

Discuss the choices you make, then work together to create a new final couplet, perhaps using the final line as it stands. Less able writers might contribute single words or phrases to a given format.

● Record a reading of the poem. Work together to decide what tone of voice should be used to convey the mysteriousness of the rider.

● Ask a group to list some questions they would like to ask the rider. When they have created their list, ask one of them to take the role of the rider and let the rest of the group question him. Encourage the group to reflect on the answers they were given – were they plausible, imaginative?

Extension/further reading

Ask readers to select poems from *A Child's Garden of Verses*. Encourage comparisons with 'Windy Nights'.

4: 2: T4: to understand how the use of expressive and descriptive language can, e.g. create moods, arouse expectations, build tension, describe attitudes or emotions

4: 2: T7: to identify different patterns of rhyme and verse in poetry, e.g. rhyming couplets; alternate line rhymes and to read these aloud effectively

repetition of 'whenever' reinforces how often this happens

we get no detail, not even an adjective

assonance builds up the sound picture

again, repetition suggests that this goes on and on

punctuation helps reader keep rhythm

typically 'poetic' sentence structure

WINDY NIGHTS

Whenever the moon and stars are set, **1**
  Whenever the wind is high, **2**
All night long in the dark and wet, **3**
  A man goes riding by. **4**
Late in the night when the fires are out, **5**
Why does he gallop and gallop about? **6**

Whenever the trees are crying aloud,
  And ships are tossed at sea,
By, on the highway, low and loud,
  By at a gallop goes he.
By at the gallop he goes, and then
By he comes back at the gallop again.

Robert Louis Stevenson

1st and 3rd lines rhyme

2nd and 4th lines rhyme

final couplet also rhymes in each verse

powerful use of personification

further examples of assonance

the lack of detail and the repetition makes this seem very mysterious

4: 2: T11: to write poetry based on the structure and/or style of poems read, e.g. taking account of vocabulary, archaic expressions, patterns of rhyme

4: 2: S4: to recognise how commas, connectives and full stops are used to join separate clauses; to identify where each is effective

The Listeners by Walter de la Mare

Background

Walter de la Mare is a widely anthologised poet who wrote extensively for children. 'The Listeners' is written in a deliberately archaic style, it sounds older than 'Windy Nights', although it was written much later. There are similarities of subject – this too includes a ghostly element.

Shared reading and discussing the text

● Read the poem a number of times. Notice that, like 'Windy Nights', it creates a mysterious atmosphere.

● Help the children to identify the mystery by focusing on the setting. Ask what sort of place the Traveller has come to. Look for lines that give information about the setting. Establish that it is a lonely house, set in or near a forest.

● Now focus on the Traveller. Ask the children to read the poem again, then work in pairs to find out two things about the Traveller. (For example, he has ridden to a lonely house at night and knocked on the door, he seems to be keeping a promise, he rides away again.)

● Point out the *phantom listeners*, link them to the poem's title and re-read the next seven lines. Ask the children to speculate about who the listeners might be. Is there evidence that they are ghosts? Are they frightening?

● As you read them, ask the children to act out the lines where the Traveller knocks on the door. Ask if the Traveller knows that there are 'phantoms' in the house. Mark lines in the poem that support the view that he does.

● Focus now on the language of the poem. Explain that there are old-fashioned words or expressions in the poem, such as *dwelt* and *smote*. Can the class explain what they mean? List other examples and encourage the children to have a go at defining them. Ask why the poet might have used these unfamiliar words. (He wanted the poem to sound old fashioned.)

● Point out some instances of alliteration in the text, such as *forest's ferny floor*. Can the children find other examples? What effect do they have? (They help to create atmosphere.)

● Look at the penultimate line. Discuss the image of silence rushing like the sea to fill in the gap where the Traveller had been. Use a thesaurus to find synonyms for *surge*. Which meaning fits best? Ask the children to explore what this suggests, for example that the house exists as a kind of ghost house that is never visited, the Traveller interrupts this, but in the end the ghostly state returns.

Activities

● Give a group the first eight lines of the poem and ask them to work out the rhyme pattern. Then give them the rest of the poem to check. Ask them to discuss the half-rhyme of *stone* and *gone* at the end of the poem. (Same spelling pattern, but different phonemes.)

● Organise the class into groups of three to discuss these three questions:

1. Who or what were the *phantom listeners*? What were they doing there?

2. What had made the Traveller come to the house so late at night?

3. What happened to the house and the Traveller afterwards?

Each group is to invent a story that answers the questions. Number the members of each group 1, 2 and 3 and then ask number 1s to form a new group of three with other number 1s. Do the same with 2s and 3s. Ask the new groups to tell each other how the story their original group invented explains the questions.

● Ask a group to make a glossary of the old-fashioned words you collected from the poem, checking their meanings in a dictionary.

● Tell groups to check through the poem again, marking words, phrases and sentences that they particularly like. Ask them to make a table to record their favourite lines, with a brief explanation of why they like it.

Extension/further reading

'Trespassers will…' by Philip Gross and 'The New House' by Edward Thomas in *Otherworlds: Poems of the Mysterious* compiled by Judith Nicholls (Faber and Faber) have similar themes.

4: 2: T4: to understand how the use of expressive and descriptive language can, e.g. create moods, arouse expectations, build tension, describe attitudes or emotions

4: 2: T5: to understand the use of figurative language in poetry

this question is repeated; the whole poem seems to answer 'yes', but no one speaks to the Traveller

THE LISTENERS

narrative poem – story being told

alliteration creates a sound picture

means 'hit'; deliberate use of an old-fashioned verb

"Is there anybody there?" said the Traveller,
Knocking on the moonlit door;
And his horse in the silence champed the grasses
Of the forest's ferny floor:
And a bird flew up out of the turret,
Above the Traveller's head:
And he smote upon the door again a second time;
"Is there anybody there?" he said.
But no one descended to the Traveller;
No head from the leaf-fringed sill
Leaned over and looked into his grey eyes,
Where he stood perplexed and still.
But only a host of phantom listeners
That dwelt in the lone house then,
Stood listening in the quiet of the moonlight
To that voice from the world of men:
Stood thronging the faint moonbeams on the dark stair,
That goes down to the empty hall,
Harkening in an air stirred and shaken
By the lonely Traveller's call.
And he felt in his heart their strangeness,
Their stillness answering his cry,
While his horse moved, cropping the dark turf,
'Neath the starred and leafy sky;
For he suddenly smote on the door, even
Louder, and lifted his head:–
"Tell them I came, and no one answered,
That I kept my word," he said.
Never the least stir made the listeners,
Though every word he spake
Fell echoing through the shadowiness of the still house
From the one man left awake:
Ay, they heard his foot upon the stirrup,
And the sound of iron on stone,
And how the silence surged softly backward,
When the plunging hoofs were gone.

Walter de la Mare

rhyme

Traveller is not described, so is rather mysterious

suggests that the listeners are of another world, do not seem frightening, just strange

picks up the title; we know almost nothing about the listeners – we get no description; who are they? why do they just listen?

'listening'; again deliberately archaic

Traveller seems to be aware of something inside the house

he seems to have made a promise to someone to come to this lonely house; no details are given though

alliteration again

strong metaphor – the silence 'surges' like the sea back into the space left by the Traveller

4: 2: T6: to identify clues which suggest poems are older, e.g. language use, vocabulary, archaic words

4: 2: T7: to identify different patterns of rhyme and verse in poetry, e.g. rhyming couplets, alternate line rhymes and to read these aloud effectively

4: 2: W11: to understand that vocabulary changes over time

The Way Through the Woods

by Rudyard Kipling

Background

Like the other classic poems included here, this is a poem of atmosphere rather than action. Again, there is an element of the ghost story to it. Rudyard Kipling was a Victorian writer who wrote *The Jungle Book* and 'If', one of the best-loved English poems.

Shared reading and discussing the text

● Explain to the children that they will find many of the same features of repetition, alliteration and rhyme as in the other mysterious poems. Give them the opportunity to read and discuss in pairs, before asking them to mark the text where they identify these features.

● Check children's appreciation of the poem by asking them to explain the meaning of key words or lines, such as *coppice*, *Weather and rain have undone it again*. Ask them to share their understanding.

● Focus on the poem's setting, asking children to find evidence to prove or disprove the statements you make about the poem. Perhaps: *The poem is set in a city, on a busy road; No you're right it is set in a wood, but the path is well used by lots of villagers; You can walk along this path and never be aware of anyone or anything.*

● Examine the second verse. Point out the time of day and ask why this might be important. (Twilight is a time of shadows, when things appear strange or uncertain.) Ask what a visitor to a wood at this time of evening might hear. Check the children understand the significance of the noises – it implies that there are people moving up and down the road.

● Ask the children to work in pairs to discover how the poet explains these noises, particularly in the last three lines. Take any ideas, however tentative. The people seem to be travelling down a long-forgotten road.

● Highlight the last line of the poem. Why does the poet reinforce that there is no road? Explain that the poem is actually a very gentle ghost story, where the ghosts just move along where

the road used to be, as they did when they were alive.

Activities

● Ask a group to create a storyboard that a film director might use to map out a short film or video of this poem. Limit them to four to six images only and encourage them to identify key moments to be emphasised. They might note details of suitable sound effects that could accompany each of the images.

● Prepare a false interpretation of the poem, for example *'The Way Through the Woods' is about a child who walks down an old road in a forest and meets lots of ghosts and is scared by them.* Ask children to work together to gather evidence, perhaps as a series of bullet points, to explain why the interpretation is incorrect.

● Tape a deliberately poor reading of this poem, perhaps by reading it too quickly. Ask a group to criticise the reading and make their own recording, thinking how best to bring out the mystery of the poem. They could also record readings of the other two classic poems and script a link between each one.

● Return to the features of rhyme, repetition and alliteration which are common to these classic poems. Ask them why all three poets might have used these features. What effect do they have? You might talk to them about how the setting and the atmosphere is created by a careful use of language that emphasises sound rather than action or description. Encourage children to read the poems aloud to emphasise this point.

Extension/further reading

Ask the children to look at all three classic poems and make a preference chart, identifying what they like and dislike about each one.

Caliban's speech *Be not afeared; the isle is full of noises...* from Act 3, Scene II of Shakespeare's *The Tempest* makes similar reference to mysterious but unthreatening noises.

4: 2: T4: to understand how the use of expressive and descriptive language can, e.g. create moods, arouse expectations, build tension, describe attitudes or emotions

4: 2: T6: to identify clues which suggest poems are older, e.g. language use, vocabulary, archaic words

THE WAY THROUGH THE WOODS

They shut the road through the woods
Seventy years ago.
Weather and rain have undone it again,
And now you would never know
There was once a road through the woods
Before they planted the trees.
It is underneath the coppice and heath,
And the thin anemones.
Only the keeper sees
That, where the ring-dove broods,
And the badgers roll at ease,
There was once a road through the woods.

Yet, if you enter the woods
Of a summer evening late,
When the night-air cools on the trout-ringed pools
Where the otter whistles his mate,
(They fear not men in the woods,
Because they see so few)
You will hear the beat of a horse's feet,
And the swish of a skirt in the dew,
Steadily cantering through
The misty solitudes,
As though they perfectly knew
The old lost road through the woods…
But there is no road through the woods.

Rudyard Kipling

in the sense of removing all signs of the road; visitors now would not know there had been a road

near-repetition of this line in last line of verse and last line of poem

every 2nd and 4th line rhyme

the keeper, because he walks this way often, can see the signs of where the road once was

suggests that this is not just a quiet place that few people visit; sets up mystery

a very tranquil, calm scene

the animals rarely see humans, so have no fear, adding to the mystery of the 'human' noises

ghostly sounds of people using the road

alliteration of rustling 's' sounds

4: 2: T7: to identify different patterns of rhyme and verse in poetry, e.g. choruses, rhyming couplets, alternate line rhymes, and to read these aloud effectively

Rivers

Background

This extract is from the *Oxford Children's Encyclopedia*. It gives information and provides a detailed explanation of how something happens, so includes features such as a general opening statement followed by a series of logical steps explaining why something occurs. Explanation texts typically use a simple present tense, time and causal connectives, and often use questions in their sub-headings. This extract is intended to be compared with the following one, 'Fact File', but you may want to collect other texts about rivers and the water cycle. Although specialist vocabulary is defined in the text, a glossary might also be helpful.

Shared reading and discussing the text

● Read the text, checking understanding of vocabulary such as *tributaries* and *drainage basin*. Then re-read it, paragraph by paragraph.

● For the first paragraph, ask children to find out how streams form rivers. Give opportunities for discussion, then ask for contributions.

● Use the information in the second paragraph to create a simple labelled diagram. Label the river, the tributaries, the sea and the drainage basin, involving the children as much as possible.

● Point out the second sub-heading and contrast it with the first one. Ask the children to predict what information they will be given in the next paragraph. (How water cuts through land.)

● Re-read the second section and ask the children in pairs to make notes, ideally using a white board, on how valleys and gorges are made. Remind them that notes should be brief and include only essential information. Set them a word limit as a constraint (say 20 to 25 words). Discuss contributions and agree a version, for example *Rivers cut through the land because the force of water and the sediment it carries make wider and deeper channels*.

● Now read the last paragraph. Ask the children to identify three reasons why rivers wear away land more quickly in some places than in others.

Activities

● Ask a group to compare the explanation of technical terms, such as *tributaries*, with that given in other information sources you have. Are the explanations correct and helpful? After checking, the children might create a glossary to support class work about rivers.

● Ask a group to turn the first or third paragraph into labelled diagrams. They should use the information given to make an accurate and careful representation.

● Set a group to research the Grand Canyon for a presentation. They should link their presentation to the text's explanation of how rivers wear away land.

● Work with children who find note-taking difficult. Remind them that when taking notes, you are trying to write down only the essential information. Show them how to use headings, remove examples, abbreviate text and highlight key words.

● Work with a group to use diagrams as a means of note-taking. This might include demonstrating how to represent words visually to help explain or remember their meaning, for example, enlarging the 'v' of *valley*: *A Valley is made by a river…*; writing *tributary* a number of times as small lines which join up with *river* written as a larger line; writing *sediment* out of dots to represent the stones and sand of which it is made up. Ask the group to invent their own visual representations of key vocabulary.

● Ask an able group to re-read the text and then write out a set of research questions, focused on what else they would like to know about rivers. Then set them the task of finding out the answers to their own questions.

Extension/further reading

Taking the basic question in this extract, *What is a river?*, compare answers and explanations from other information sources. Is the information consistent? Get the children to compare both content and presentation features, perhaps by developing a tick list to identify features present in particular texts.

4: 2: T17: to scan texts in print or on screen to locate key words or phrases, useful headings and key sentences and to use these as a tool for summarising text

4: 2: T18: to mark extracts by annotating and by selecting key headings, words or sentences, or alternatively, noting these

a question is a useful sub-heading – implies that the text below it will provide an answer

an opening statement that briefly explains the topic developed in the paragraphs below

technical vocabulary is explained

Rivers

What is a river?

A river is formed when water flows naturally between clearly defined banks. The water comes from rain or snow. When rain falls or snow melts, some of the water runs off the land down the steepest slope, forming trickles of water in folds of the land. These trickles eventually merge together to form streams, which join up to form rivers. The streams which join the main river are called tributaries. Some of the rain-water also sinks into the ground, and seeps down through the rocks until it meets a layer of rock which cannot hold any more water. Then the water runs out at the surface to form a spring.

A river gets bigger and bigger as it flows towards the sea, because more and more tributaries join it. The area of land which supplies a river with water is called its drainage basin.

Rivers wear away rocks

Rivers cut into the land and create valleys and gorges. Rushing water has tremendous force. A cubic metre of water weighs a tonne. Water can split rocks just by pounding them. But more important is the load of sediment (stones and sand) the river carries. Rocks and soil are swept along by fast-flowing water, scouring the river bed and banks. Large boulders are bounced along the river bed, scouring out a deeper and deeper channel.

The rate at which the water wears away the land depends partly on how hard the rock is, and partly on the slope of the river. The steeper it is, the greater its power to erode (wear away). Where the land is rising or the sea-level is falling, rivers can cut down through the rocks very fast. The mountains of the Grand Canyon in the United States were rising as the Colorado River cut down through it. Today, the river has cut a gorge 1.5 kilometres (1 mile) deep.

quite detailed explanation of how rivers are formed

sub-heading allows reader to predict what information will follow

specialist vocabulary explained

great deal of information given in each paragraph

4: 2: T21: to make short notes, e.g. by abbreviating ideas, selecting key words, listing or in diagrammatic form

4: 2: W3: to use independent spelling strategies, including using word banks, dictionaries

Fact File by Richard Stephens

141

Background

This information text includes elements of a report, which describes the way something is. Typically, reports include a general opening, followed by technical information and description. They are usually written in the present tense and are non-chronological. This text contrasts with the previous encyclopedia extract in approach and presentation.

Shared reading and discussing the text

● Explain that this text about rivers is different from the previous one. Ask the children to read it independently and note some of the obvious differences, for example greater use of sub-headings, includes facts about rivers rather than an explanation of their formation, greater use of examples. Ask the children to skim the text to gain an overall impression of it.

● Model how to scan a text, looking for key words to decide where to read more carefully. Say that you want to find out about the widest river in the world and suggest sub-headings are useful. Read these aloud, pointing out the significance of *Widest river*. Check that no other sub-heading is more relevant, then return to this one. Explain that once you have found the right section you will read more carefully to identify the information you need. Read the section aloud and underline how you have answered your original question.

● In pairs, ask the children to decide where to find out about waterfalls. Remind them to use the sub-headings. Once they have all located the place, ask them a question based on that section. Repeat the exercise with other questions to let the children practise scanning.

● Look again at the sub-headings. Explain that they are deliberately brief – only two words each, but many of the sub-headings could be expressed as questions. *Most water* could become *Which river carries the most water?* Ask pairs to turn the sub-heading *Largest delta* into a question. To do this, they should read the information in that section and consider what question it is answering. Explain that questions

are often used in information books as a way of organising material.

● Recap work on representing information through diagrams and pictures. Highlight the *Longest rivers* section and ask how this information could be represented as a diagram. Work through some ideas, or model how a graph gives information. Give the graph a title, such as *The longest rivers in each continent*. Calibrate the vertical axis mark in divisions of 1000km, up to 7000km, and then mark off the rivers by name along the horizontal axis.

Activities

● Ask a group to use an atlas to check information given in the *Largest delta* section. They could find a map of India and Bangledesh, locate the delta and then follow the route of the two contributory rivers.

● Ask children to list comparisons between this text and the one from the *Oxford Children's Encyclopedia*. This comparison chart might be as simple as a two-column table, headed *Similarities* and *Differences*. Ask the children to compare both the information and the presentation. More able children might be able to extend this work by comparing a third text.

● Able children could combine information from both sources, to create a poster or leaflet about rivers, for younger children. If possible, show them an example. Their poster might explain how rivers develop, and include an *Amazing facts about rivers* section. Encourage them to consider the presentation of information, for example using headings and diagrams. After completion, question them about how best to present information.

Extension/further reading

Take the sub-headings in the extract and use them to research rivers in England, Scotland, Wales or Ireland, comparing them with the rivers mentioned in the extract.

Rivers by Terry Jennings (Belitha Press) would be a good text for more able readers or as a source text for guided reading.

4: 2: T17: to scan texts in print or on screen to locate key words or phrases, useful headings and key sentences and to use these as a tool for summarising text

4: 2: T18: to mark extracts by annotating and by selecting key headings, words or sentences, or alternatively, noting these

Fact File

Longest rivers

The longest river in each continent is:
Africa: Nile 6,670km
S. America: Amazon 6,450km
Asia: Yangtze 6,300km
N. America: Mississippi-Missouri 6,210km
Europe: Volga 3,690 km
Australasia: Murray 3,220km

Most water

Out of all the water that rivers pour into the world's oceans, one fifth comes from the Amazon. It pours out as much in a day as the Thames does in a year. The Amazon pushes back the salt water of the Atlantic for 150km and stains the ocean brown for 300km.

Widest river

The Amazon is so wide that there is an island at its mouth as big as Switzerland. The Amazon is deep, too. Ocean-going ships can travel up the river for 3,200km, right through Brazil to the jungle port of Iquitos in Peru.

Largest delta

The triangular mouth of the Nile reminded ancient geographers of the Greek letter delta (Δ). As a result, a river mouth, where silt has built up, forming a triangular maze of islands and channels, is known as a delta.

The world's largest delta is partly in India and partly in Bangladesh. It is formed by two rivers, the Ganges and the Brahmaputra, and covers an area the size of Scotland. Other famous rivers with deltas include the Mississippi, the Yellow River and the Rhine.

Tidal bores

A rapidly rising ocean flood tide can create a wave that rushes upstream from a river mouth. About 60 of the world's rivers have tidal bores.

The bore of China's Qiantang River can be 7.5 metres high and can travel at 25km per hour. The Amazon's bore is often 4.5 metres high and 16km wide at the river's mouth.

Highest waterfall

The world's highest waterfalls are the Angel Falls, on the Churun River in Venezuela. From top to bottom, they are almost 1km high, 18 times higher than Niagara Falls.

short sub-headings used throughout to organise information

each paragraph gives facts relevant to the heading, it does not explain *why*

some background

different form of presentation – a list of names with each length given

comparison with the Thames helps British readers understand the size of the Amazon

lots of numbers included, particularly distances

there is enough information given here to draw a diagram

short statements of fact

4: 2: T21: to make short notes, e.g. by abbreviating ideas, selecting key words, listing or in diagrammatic form

4: 2: T23: to collect information from a variety of sources and present it in one simple format, e.g. wall chart, labelled diagram

Brains

Background
This text is another from the *Oxford Children's Encyclopedia* and could be read alongside the contrasting 'Bulging brain basics'. Explanations tell us how something works or explain the processes involved in a natural event or phenomenon. They include a general opening statement, followed by a series of logical steps. Usually they are written in the present tense and use time and causal connectives.

Shared reading and discussing the text
● Read the text with the children and clarify any unfamiliar vocabulary, ideally by creating a glossary. Demonstrate how to use context to get an approximate meaning.
● Revise the purpose and form of explanation texts, using a checklist of features:

Features of explanation text	Can I find an example in this text?
Title to indicate content	
General opening statement	
Series of logical steps	
Steps continue until the explanation is complete	
Written in simple present tense	
Uses connectives that signal time, eg *then*, *next*	
Uses causal connectives, eg *because, so, while, this causes*	
May use diagrams or illustrations to aid the explanation	

● Re-read the text. Ask the children to discuss whether the piece includes a helpful title and begins with a general opening statement. Mark these features on the text.
● Re-read the passage to see whether logical steps are a feature. (It uses two separate sets of logically constructed information, organised under sub-headings.)
● Re-read the first paragraph. Agree a new sub-heading for this section, for example *What is the brain?* Do the same for the second paragraph, for example *What brain cells do.*

● Point out the sub-heading *Information from the senses*. Ask the children what they would expect to find in this section. They should re-read these paragraphs to check. Explain that effective sub-headings help a reader to know what a section is about. Ask the children to sum up the important information from one of the paragraphs in a limited number of words.
● Return to the checklist. Ask the class to check through the other features listed. Identify the verbs and check what tense they are written in. Discuss how a sentence would sound if it were written in the past tense.
● Now look at the connectives. Encourage the children to underline some of the connectives in the paragraph beginning *Using information…* (*so, but, and, if*). Discuss whether these are time connectives or causal connectives (which signal that one things leads to another). Tick the boxes in the table accordingly.

Activities
● Let a group research different sources for pictures of the brain and then make a labelled diagram to accompany the text.
● A group could use a dictionary to check the definitions of words that you collected earlier, adding to or changing the definition as necessary.
● Re-read the text with weaker readers. Repeat your discussion of explanation texts. Use the glossary to revisit unfamiliar vocabulary. Check their knowledge of strategies to use when they face difficulties, for example blending phonemes, reading on and reading back. Let them read independently and monitor their reading. Return to the text by revisiting difficult sections. Ask the children to explain how they overcame any problems.

Extension/further reading
Provide an able group with another explanation text, for example from an encyclopedia, and ask them to use the checklist on it. How many features can they find? Ask them to compare the two texts and report back during a plenary.

4: 2: T18: to mark extracts by annotating and by selecting key headings, words or sentences, or alternatively, noting these

4: 2: T19: to identify how and why paragraphs are used to organise and sequence information

title to identify what the text is about

general opening statement

passive voice

paragraph written in logical steps to show how brain cells function

sub-heading

explanation texts are typically written in the present tense

Brains

Most animals have a brain that controls thoughts and actions. The brain consists of many nerve cells. Each cell is connected to many other nerve cells, some of which pass information from sense organs, such as ears or eyes, into the brain, while others are connected to nerves that lead from the brain to muscles.

Most of the brain cells in mammals connect to other brain cells and process incoming information, carry out thought processes and make elaborate decisions. Even smaller and less intelligent animals, such as bees, can remember where their hive is and calculate the time of day.

Information from the senses

The sense organs pass information to different parts of the brain as a series of nerve impulses which act as signals. These may be simple signals, giving information about what part of the body has been touched, or a complex series of signals using thousands of nerve cells to let you to see the shape of letters and read the words on this page.

Using information from different parts of the brain, an animal sends

signals to its muscles so that it can move in a controlled way. Some movements, such as a single kick, do not require much control, but walking and flying require exact control of the muscles. You would fall over and bump into things if you could not adjust your muscles continually

The brain receives and processes signals from the sense organs to make these adjustments. It connects with nerves in the spinal cord which runs down from the head, inside the backbone. Nerves from the spinal cord connect with muscles, while other nerves from sense cells in the skin and muscles connect back into the spinal cord. Other nerves connect the spinal cord back to the brain.

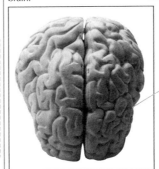

not all technical terms are explained, although reader does get a general idea of the function of nerve cells

connectives link one idea with another

this clear explanation could be used to draw a diagram

photograph helps reader to visualise

example to illustrate the importance of brain cells

4: 2: T20: to identify from the examples the key features of explanatory texts:
- purpose: to explain a process or to answer a question
- structure: introduction, followed by sequential explanation, organised into paragraphs
- language features: usually present tense; use of connectives of time and cause and effect; use of passive voice
- presentation: use of diagrams, other illustrations

4: 2: W1: to read and spell words through blending phonemes for reading

4: 2: W3: to use independent spelling strategies, including building from words with similar patterns, using word banks, dictionaries

4: 2: S4: to recognise how commas, connectives and full stops are used to join separate clauses

Bulging brain basics by Nick Arnold

Background

This extract is from a book in the *Horrible Science* series. Like the text from the *Oxford Children's Encyclopedia* it explains how the brain works and includes some characteristic features of an explanation text, but the style of writing and presentation are very different; it is intended to entertain as well as inform.

Shared reading and discussing the text

● Introduce this extract by explaining the links with 'Brains': same subject, both explanation texts. Ask the children to try to identify how 'Bulging brain basics' is different as you read it. (For example, the vocabulary is far less technical and more colloquial, the tone is humorous.)

● Ask if any children know the *Horrible Science* books or the similar *Horrible Histories*. Ask the class to re-read the extract and identify features that indicate the text was written to entertain as well as inform. (The direct addresses to the reader, the jokes, the use of child-friendly terms like *guts* rather than more biologically accurate terms.) Reinforce this by making a direct comparison with 'Brains'.

● Use the explanation checklist from the previous text to analyse the features of this one. Alternatively, recall how explanations should move from a general introductory statement to a series of points about the thing being explained. Ask if this is true of the section headed *What's your brain for?*.

● Re-read the opening sentences of the first three paragraphs and use them to summarise the paragraphs. Ask the children if they notice any similarity between the three key sentences. Underline *The brain* in the first paragraph and ask the children to find similar phrases in the next two. Underline these too. Next, ask children to look for other occasions where a sentence starts with *The brain* or a similar construction. Explain that Nick Arnold has organised his information by using a similar construction many times. Ask if the children find the repetition boring. (Probably not because the rest of the writing is so vivid.)

● Introduce the second section of the piece, *Inside the bulging brain*. Here the extract is more like an information sheet than an explanation, although the *Disgusting details* do explain why the brain needs blood. Help the children to identify the difference between information and explanation by asking them to identify through discussion where the author gives them facts and where he uses these facts to explain how or why something works.

Activities

● Give a group the explanation checklist and ask them to complete a thorough analysis of this text. More able readers could write down an example or underline the features in the text.

● An able group might analyse this extract from *Bulging Brains*, using the checklist and then compare it with 'Brains'. They could draw up a similarities and differences chart.

● Introduce the text briefly and let the children read it independently, with 'Brains'. Afterwards, ask them to make notes about which of the two texts they prefer and why. They might work up their notes into a brief paragraph using the introductory phrase *I prefer... because...*

● Ask a group to identify five pieces of information they have learned about the brain from both extracts. Work with them to construct a brief explanatory paragraph about the brain; what it is, how it functions and what it does. Then ask them to begin their own draft. At regular intervals as they write, encourage children to use the checklist to make sure the features identified are included. Make changes as necessary to make the explanation clearer and more precise.

Extension/further reading

Compare this text with the extract from *The Terrible Tudors* (see page 18). Although by different authors and about very different subjects, are there any similarities of style?

Blood, Bones and Body Bits, another book from the *Horrible Science* series includes lots more rather gruesome information!

4: 2: T9: to recognise how certain types of texts are targeted at particular readers; to identify intended audience

4: 2: T18: to mark extracts by annotating and by selecting key headings, words or sentences, or alternatively, noting these

4: 2: T19: to identify how and why paragraphs are used to organise and sequence information

4: 2: T25: to write explanations of a process, using conventions identified through reading

question used as sub-heading

each paragraph's opening line acts as a kind of summary of the rest of the paragraph

humorous simile

unusual adjective for an explanation text – indicates text is written for children and to entertain

alliteration

gives more factual information than explanation

this paragraph does not explain how the brain functions, but tells what it does and why it is important

change of style – list and diagram

unusual verb – makes the brain sound like a voracious monster!

question and response directly address reader

unexpected noun used for comic effect and to relate to child audience

BULGING BRAIN BASICS

What's your brain for?

The brain is the part of your body that tells you what's going on around you. You can use your brain to order your body around and even to order everybody else around. But there's much more to your brain. Much, much more.

Inside your brain are your precious memories, your dreams, your hopes for the future and the knowledge of everything you love and care about. In your brain you can sense lovely smells and tastes and colours. Your brain helps you feel great and happy about life and that's the good side. But your brain also creates horrible fears and worries that can make you miserable.

Your brain makes the thoughts and feelings that make your personality. Your brain turns your body from a living object into you the person. Without a brain you'd be as dead as a dodo's tombstone, so it's good to know that you've got your very own bulging brain right now between your ears... hopefully.

Inside the bulging brain

Still want to be a brain surgeon? Excellent! Now you've found out a bit about what the bulging brain does, you're ready to check out how it works...

Bet you never knew!
Your brain weighs less than 1.3 kg – that's a little less than the weight of a large bag of sugar or the weight of all the germs swarming in your guts.

Bulging fact file

NAME: The brain

BASIC FACTS: The brain is made up of three main parts: FOREBRAIN, MID-BRAIN, HIND-BRAIN.

Each area is made up of smaller bits with different jobs. (For more details see page 32–35.)

DISGUSTING DETAILS: The brain needs energy from the sugar and oxygen carried in the blood. So it sucks in about 750 ml (one pint) of the red stuff every minute. All this hot blood gives out lots of heat – that's why your brain is the hottest part of your body.

4: 2: T20: to identify from the examples the key features of explanatory texts:

- purpose: to explain a process or to answer a question
- structure: introduction, followed by sequential explanation, organised into paragraphs
- language features: usually present tense; use of connectives of time and cause and effect; use of passive voice
- presentation: use of diagrams, other illustrations

Bella's Den

by Berlie Doherty

Extract 1

Background
This extract is the opening from a short novel. The book tells the story of a child moving from an urban area to a new home in the countryside and making a new friend. Later in the story, in Bella's den, the two girls witness the magical sight of a fox family playing at twilight.

Shared reading and discussing the text
● Tell the children that this extract is the opening to a novel. Read the first paragraph, with the last sentence covered. Ask the children to predict what the sentence could be. Re-read the paragraph, identifying the sentences that mention horses and the verbs that suggest horse riding. Then reveal the final sentence and compare it with the children's suggestions.

● Read the second paragraph. Point out the personal pronoun, *I*. Explain that this is a first-person narrative; the story is told from the narrator's point of view, so we only hear about what the narrator knows or understands.

● Ask what new information has been gained from the second paragraph, for example that Bella is the narrator's only friend in the area. State that you would infer that the narrator has only recently moved to the countryside. Ask the children to work in pairs to find any evidence from the text that supports this view.

● Discuss how the narrator might feel as a new child in the area. As well as encouraging the children to draw on their own experiences of moving home, for example, point out the text references that suggest the narrator is lonely.

● Explain that the first paragraph takes the reader straight into the action, then the second fills in the background. Now read paragraph 3. How has the story moved on? Can the children suggest a sub-title for this paragraph? (Perhaps *Falling out*, *Bella's disappearance*.)

● Point out that the second and third paragraphs sound like a child talking, and ask the children how the writer achieves this. After discussion, reinforce their understanding of the technique by identifying the use of the personal pronoun, the mix of short and long sentences, colloquial language and exaggeration. Point out how this is also demonstrated in the opening paragraph in the make-believe of the bicycles as horses.

● Ask the children to speculate on what Bella's secret might be. Then point out the title of the story. Could the title be a clue to the secret?

Activities
● Children could begin a reading journal, to collect notes about what they have noticed in the story so far and make predictions. They could also have a page about Bella to list everything they know about Bella at this point.

● Re-read the extract, clarifying beforehand any challenging vocabulary and reminding the children of useful strategies, such as to re-read a paragraph slowly. They could then work in groups to discuss and list reasons why Bella might not want to tell the narrator her secret.

● Interview the two main characters to find out more about them by hot-seating. Use prepared or spontaneous questions, depending on the confidence of the children. After questioning, ask the children to reflect on what they have found out. Get them to check and discuss how plausible and justifiable the new information is.

● Help a group to compose a letter sent from the narrator to a friend from her old town. Brainstorm ideas for content, then work together on structure and capturing the right tone of voice for the narrator.

● In shared writing, compose a final paragraph to complete the chapter. Demonstrate how to start, for example *Then one day...*, talking through the choices you make and asking for contributions. Consider alternatives and decide together which suggestions sound the most appropriate, and why. Remind the children to maintain the use of the first-person narrator.

Extension/further reading
After examining a few examples of book blurbs, ask the children to compose one for *Bella's Den*. Advise them that you want their blurbs to encourage other children to read the novel.

4: 3: T1: to identify social, moral or cultural issues in stories, e.g. the dilemmas faced by characters or the moral of the story, and to discuss how the characters deal with them; to locate evidence in text

is this the secret?

sustained metaphor

action right from 1st sentences

use of personal pronouns; 1st-person narrative

2nd paragraph fills in background information

realistic – sounds like children talking

3rd paragraph tells us more about the girls' relationship and about Bella

comic mix of reality and metaphor

at this stage, there is no hint as to what it is

not clear at this point that the horses are imaginary

narrator not identified so far

illustration of how, by keeping back a piece of information, a writer can control how reader reacts

Bella takes time to be sure of people

moving to the country has left the narrator isolated

remember Polly is a dog!

how we make, keep and lose friends is at the heart of the story

Bella is strong willed and independent

Bella knows the countryside well

BELLA'S DEN

Extract 1

WE ALWAYS CAME down the lane on our horses. We galloped faster and faster, mud flying round us, with Polly the sheepdog leaping behind. We had to rein the horses in really hard when we got to the farm gate in case they tried to leap over and sent us flying. Then we tethered them to the fence. Bella's was called Lightning and mine was called Splash. We had to leave them at the fence because they'd never make it through the next bit. They weren't really horses, you see. They were bikes.

I'd been playing horses with Bella for weeks before she told me about the next bit. She'd never told anyone else about it, and she had to get to know me pretty well before she told me. I had millions of friends where I lived before, all in my street, and all the way down town to school. But here there was only one person to play with for miles, and that was Bella. And Polly, but you couldn't count on her because she wasn't even allowed out with us at lambing time. So it was a good job I got on with Bella.

I didn't always, though. She had an annoying habit of disappearing. Sometimes, if we had an argument about whose horse had won or whose turn it was to close the farm gate, she would just stand there with her face closing up as if she was thinking, "I don't have to play with you, you know." I'd go back to shut the gate and she'd disappear. I just didn't know how she did it. Polly went too. It was no use waiting for them or shouting their names. I'd just have to wheel my horse back home and sit watching telly, like I used to do when we first came here. She had a secret, Bella had, and she was pretty good at keeping it.

4: 3: T3: to understand how paragraphs or chapters are used to collect, order and build up ideas

4: 3: T11: to explore the main issues of a story by writing a story about a dilemma and the issues it raises for the character

Bella's Den

by Berlie Doherty

Extract 2

145

Background

This second extract begins the day after Bella and the narrator had watched the fox playing with her cubs. It explores the issues of consideration of wild animals, and loyalty, misunderstanding and how different people interpret things in different ways.

Shared reading and discussing the text

● Remind the children of the previous extract. Explain that the sight of the foxes playing had been an almost magical experience for the girls and that the narrator was very excited about what she had seen. To understand why the narrator feels the turmoil revealed in this extract, it is important the children grasp that farmers would view foxes as pests. Ask why people have different opinions about foxes.

● Read the text and ask the children to identify two different views about foxes in the passage (Bella's and the farmer's.) Give the children the opportunity to discuss their own opinions.

● Explain that the narrator is terribly upset by what happens. Ask some children to act out the first paragraph, whilst the rest of the class focus on whether the acting fully captures the narrator's excitement. Repeat the exercise, with different children taking on the roles.

● Create a tableau of the next paragraph, where Bella and the farmer enter. Ask the children what the farmer would want to know and why. What might Bella be trying to do? Ask others what each of the characters might be thinking. 'Thought track' each of the characters in turn, where children speak as their character, saying their thoughts aloud. For example, Mum might think *What is she so excited about? And why does the farmer look like that?*

● Read on up to *I felt sick at heart*. Ask the children why everyone seems angry with the narrator. Justify ideas by reference to the text.

● Read to the end of the extract. Ask the children why Bella is so angry. Do they understand her feelings? Point out the effective simile *Her voice was like ice*, which shows how deeply Bella has been upset.

● Focus on the final paragraph, asking the children to describe how the narrator is feeling. Check their understanding of *I wished I could unsay what I'd said*. Does the narrator agree with Bella's view of foxes or the farmer's?

Activities

● Ask a group to work with both extracts from *Bella's Den*. Show them how to make an 'emotional graph' that charts the narrator's feelings since moving to the countryside, meeting Bella and seeing her den, and this confrontation with the farmer. Write the numbers 0–10 on the vertical axis, where 10 is very happy and 0 very sad. Draw a horizontal axis through the 0 point. Then choose the most important episodes and chart how happy or sad the narrator is at each of these points. Put a cross against the appropriate number and label the event. Having demonstrated this, ask the children to create their own graph with labels and compare them with others'. This comparison would make a useful discussion point and opportunity for further questioning.

● Ask the children to retell the events of the day from Bella's point of view, using a diary format. With less confident writers, give them support through guided writing and suggest an opening line, such as *I just knew that she was going to blurt something out. There she was hopping from one foot to another...*

● Working with both extracts, ask groups to dramatise a series of 'photographs' to show the key moments. Ask groups to bring particular images to life, by acting out the next few moments after the photograph was 'taken'.

Extension/further reading

Encourage the children to predict how the story might develop. In particular, how might the relationship between Bella and the narrator unfold? Ask them to write briefly their predicted conclusion. Read the end of the story.

In *The Midnight Fox* (Puffin), Betsy Byars uses a similar setting and theme: a boy from the city excited at seeing a fox and cub in the country.

4: 3: T3: to understand how paragraphs or chapters are used to collect, order and build up ideas

4: 3: T1: to identify social, moral or cultural issues in stories, e.g. the dilemmas faced by characters or the moral of the story, and to discuss how the characters deal with them; to locate evidence in text

narrator gabbles in her excitement (note short sentences and exclamation marks), without realising the impact of what she says

excellent example of how paragraphs are used to build up the drama of the situation; we can trace, for example, how Bella's actions convey her feelings

very effective presentation of narrator's regret; her desire to take back what has been said, to undo the damage

BELLA'S DEN

Extract 2

NEXT DAY I was full of it. "I've seen a fox," I said to my mum. "A real fox. And all its cubs. Three of them! They were playing!"

We were standing in the farmyard as I was telling her this. Bella had just come running towards me from her cottage, and the farmer came out of the lambing shed at the same time. He stood looking down at me.

"Where did you see this fox?" he asked me.

I waved my arm in the direction of Bella's den, and then I saw the look on her face. I couldn't believe what I'd done.

"Where exactly?" he asked.

I shook my head. "I don't remember," I stammered. Mum looked at me oddly.

"Vixen and three cubs?" the farmer asked me again.

I nodded. I couldn't look him in the eyes any more. I couldn't look at my mum. Bella had turned her back on me. The sandy earth was beginning to swirl around me, and I felt sick at heart.

"You know what foxes do, don't you?" the farmer said. "They bite lambs' heads off!"

Bella started to run back to her cottage. I ran after her. She closed her gate so I couldn't follow her in.

"You're not allowed to go to my den again," she said. Her voice was like ice. "Never, never, never."

I went up to my room, all the joy of last night drained away from me. I wished I could unsay what I'd said. I wished I could say, "It wasn't true. I didn't really see a fox," or "It wasn't over there. It was the other way, over the railway line." But it was too late.

narrator is trying to minimise the damage; to avoid giving away Bella's secret without angering the farmer and her mother

narrator feels out of control and queasy

farmer has very strong, and understandable, point of view; totally opposite to that of Bella and narrator

powerful simile – Bella's cold voice shows how angry she is about what has happened; she feels let down, betrayed

4: 3: T11: to explore the main issues of a story by writing a story about a dilemma and the issues it raises for the character

4: 3: T12: to write an alternative ending for a known story and discuss how this would change the reader's view of the characters and events of the original story

The Angel of Nitshill Road
by Anne Fine

Extract 1

Background
This story focuses on the issue of bullying. At Nitshill Road School, Penny, Mark and Marigold, are bullied by Barry Hunter. No one stood up to him until Celeste came to school. She encouraged everyone to write down all the bullying incidents in her Book of Deeds.

Shared reading and discussing the text
● Spend some time carefully discussing bullying. Ask the children, in pairs, to think of examples of bullying. How does it feel to be bullied? Why are people bullies? Handle feedback with sensitivity. Ensure that all who want to contribute can, perhaps by using a convention you have already established or a 'talk signal' that confers the right to speak.

● Move towards defining a bully, then introduce the text, for example by saying, *Children in this school are beginning to fight back against the bully by recording his actions in a special Book of Deeds.* Explain *deeds* as 'actions'.

● Read the extract and take comments. Then focus on the first four sentences (to *'No! Let me!'*). Ask the children to explain why Barry's bullying *wasn't the same* as before. They need to understand that it was different because his behaviour was being noted.

● Explore the meaning of *witness*, which is important in understanding the passage. Ask the children to define it by re-reading and checking what other words would fit. Where else have they heard the word? (Perhaps in TV programmes or newspapers about courts or the police.) Then look it up in the dictionary.

● Re-read the rest of the passage. Explain that Celeste's Book of Deeds is a bit like a diary or a police report, recording where Barry is unkind. Draw attention to the layout of the text – usually associated with non-fiction. Point out *Witnesses* again, ensuring the children understand that here it refers to these children who saw the events described.

● Ask the children to find four examples of Barry's bullying. They could highlight the incidents on the text. Point out the time-scale.

● Explain that you are going to adopt the role of Barry. Speak in role as Barry, justifying what you did, that you were only having a joke. Encourage the children to question you. Afterwards, out of role, ask them if they think Barry's excuses were reasonable.

● Focus on punctuation, particularly the speech marks for quotations of what Barry said and the use of colons to introduce a list of names. There are also a few 'asides' in brackets.

Activities
● Ask a group to draw a timeline to note Barry's behaviour on this day, from 8.45 to 10.30, placing the key details.

● The class could make a 'decision alley', by forming two lines facing each other, with a small gap in between. Ask for a volunteer to be Barry. As he walks slowly through the alley, the others explain why he should stop bullying.

● Work with a group to write the next extract from the Book of Deeds. Agree the content, for example Barry 'borrowed' someone's rubber. Discuss how you could write it: beginning with the time, identifying witnesses. Ask the group to write a sentence at a time, encouraging revision, before you move on.

● Work with a group to create Barry's version. Discuss how bullies rarely see their behaviour as unkind or unpleasant, it's 'just a laugh'. Ask the children to discuss how Barry would interpret the events as harmless. Then demonstrate how to rewrite one incident, possibly in the first person. Ask the group to rewrite other events from Barry's point of view. Stop the group regularly to read parts aloud and discuss the use of language and tone of voice.

Extension/further reading
Barry is a difficult child to control and keep out of trouble. What advice would the children give his teacher? Ask them to write a letter to Mr Fairway suggesting how to control Barry better.

The Eighteenth Emergency by Betsy Byars (Red Fox) tackles the issue of bullying with plenty of humour.

4: 3: T1: to identify social, moral or cultural issues in stories, e.g. the dilemmas faced by characters or the moral of the story, and to discuss how the characters deal with them; to locate evidence in text

4: 3: T11: to explore the main issues of a story by writing a story about a dilemma and the issues it raises for the character

Extract 1

The Angel of Nitshill Road

So Barry Hunter spent more and more of his time mucking about by himself. He was still bullying, but it wasn't the same now that each time he tried it a dozen people came running from far and wide to watch him do his worst, all shouting eagerly:

"Bags be the first witness!"

"No! Let *me*!"

There was still plenty for the Book of Deeds, though. When Celeste opened it on any page, everyone would peer over her shoulder to read it.

Thursday, 4 May

8.46   Barry Hunter wouldn't stop putting his head under Mark's toilet door when he needed to be private. He said it was "only a joke".

Witnesses: Ian. Wayne. Yusef. Mark.

8.56   Barry Hunter kept bumping into people on the way to Assembly. He said "Stop bumping" loudly to everyone he bumped, but it was really him bumping. Paul, Nesa and Zabeen say he wasn't bumping hard, he was just annoying. Wayne says his bump really hurt (and he had to bump back a bit).

Witnesses: Wayne. Zabeen. Nessa. Celeste. Kelly. Ian. Lisa. Penny. Phil. Paul. Mark. Elaine. Yusef. (And Mr Fairway gave Barry one of his looks, so he must have seen too.)

9.50   Barry Hunter sniffed near Marigold and said, "What's that horrible smell?" twice.

9.51   He did it again.

9.53   And again.

Witnesses: Lisa. Penny. Ian. Phil. Nessa. (We didn't ask Marigold because she was upset, and she doesn't sign anyway.)

10.30   Barry Hunter ruined Claire and Elaine's Fashion Show. First he hid some clothes behind the pipes, so there wasn't much time left. Then, when the people in the show were taking their turns to show their fashions off, he started booing loudly. So everyone in the show got embarrassed and wouldn't do it properly. So Mr Fairway stopped the show. (Barry Hunter wasn't the *only* one to boo, but he was *definitely* the one who started it.)

Witnesses: Claire. Elaine. Phil. Ian. Zabeen. Tracey. P.T.O.

her name is significant given the book's title (Celeste is Angel of the Stars)

diary or report format

detail in the times specified – just 10 minutes between these events

realistic child's response – Wayne can't ignore what Barry does

repeated offence

colon used to introduce a list

that people were prepared to speak out about his actions had some impact on him

someone who sees an incident and is prepared to 'testify' about it

A Book of Deeds is a religious idea, that a person's actions or sins are recorded

classic, poor, bully's excuse

but the teacher did not do anything

use of speech marks to quote Barry

4: 3: S2: to identify the common punctuation marks including commas and speech marks, and to respond to them appropriately when reading

The Angel of Nitshill Road

by Anne Fine

Extract 2

Background

This second extract is taken from near the end of the book, just before Celeste leaves the school. Her Book of Deeds, where all of Barry Hunter's unkind actions are recorded seems to have had an effect. His victims seem more confident and less lonely. It begins with Barry having kicked a box which has landed on Mark's head.

Shared reading and discussing the text

● Remind the children of their discussion of bullying and the earlier extract. In particular, recall how Celeste and her friends used the Book of Deeds to identify and stand witness to what the bully Barry Hunter had done to them.

● Now read the passage through twice. Before the second reading, ask the children to focus on a specific character – Mark, Penny or Marigold – and pay close attention to what the character does or says. Prepare a grid to collect their ideas filling in some background to the characters, for example:

Character	Earlier in the book	What he or she does or says in this extract	Does he or she feel bullied or unhappy in this extract?
Mark	Loses his temper whenever Barry comes near him		
Marigold	Doesn't have any friends, never talks to anyone		
Penny	Gets called Man Mountain by Barry		

● Let the children discuss in pairs what they notice about these characters and how, if at all, they seem to have changed. After discussion, complete column 3.

● Explain that column 3 can be completed directly from the text, but column 4 requires them to think about the 'evidence' they have

gathered. Ask them to decide whether each character is feeling bullied at this point. Press them to explain why not (for example, because they are enjoying themselves).

● Now focus on the last paragraph. What seems to be Celeste's main argument here? (Bad behaviour is only bullying if someone is upset by it.) Get the children to identify the important sentences and to try to summarise the key message first in 15 words, then 10.

● Give the class the chance to discuss Celeste's argument about bullying, perhaps as part of a plenary. Do they agree with her? Is Mark still the butt of the joke in this extract?

Activities

● Generate a short piece exploring how Barry might react to this event. Explain to the children that they are to write three paragraphs, one where Barry is trying to upset Mark, one where he notices how Mark reacts, the third when he realises that everyone is having a good time and that he can be positively involved in this. Discuss ideas for each paragraph before writing.

● Construct another extract where Barry tries to bully, but the victim finds a way of making a joke of it and turns it into fun. Agree the outline structure, particularly the ending. Act as scribe for the first paragraph, using ideas that the children contribute, and review and improve the paragraph. Work with groups in turn to construct the story, paragraph by paragraph.

● Ask the class to debate the issue of bullying, by considering why they think people bully and how best a victim can respond. Encourage them to think back to what they have read and, if appropriate, add their own ideas and experiences. Give them time to prepare one or two arguments and rehearse them in small groups, before holding the debate.

Extension/further reading

Reflect on the issues raised in *The Angel of Nitshill Road* in PSHE and citizenship lessons. If bullying can be an issue in your class, it might be appropriate to read the whole of the book.

4: 3: T1: to identify social, moral or cultural issues in stories, e.g. the dilemmas faced by characters or the moral of the story, and to discuss how the characters deal with them; to locate evidence in the text

4: 3: T3: to understand how paragraphs or chapters are used to collect, order and build up ideas

4: 3: T8: to write critically about an issue or dilemma raised in a story, explaining the problem, alternative courses of action and evaluating the writer's solution

Extract 2

The Angel of Nitshill Road

"Is he *hurt*?"

Like everyone in the playground, Mr Fairway watched Mark swivel his head round as if he were looking for radio signals.

"No," Penny heard him say. "I think he's actually making a bit of a joke of it."

Mrs Brown sounded astonished.

"Mark? Making a joke of something Barry Hunter did to him? Now there's a change!"

Just at that moment, Marigold ran up to offer Mark a guiding hand.

"Am I *dreaming*?" said Mrs Brown. "Is that *Marigold* who just ran up and joined in the game?"

"She was telling them all Bible stories yesterday," said Miss Featherstone.

"I don't believe it!" Mrs Brown said. Then, glancing down, she noticed Penny just beneath the window. Quickly, Penny ran off, pretending she was going to help Marigold steer Mark away from all the people standing around clapping his brilliant robot act. The last thing she overheard was Mrs Brown saying:

"Really, that child Penny's clothes are practically falling off her! It's time she tightened her buttons."

For the twentieth time that day, Penny hitched her skirt up and grinned. She wasn't going to tighten her buttons. Not yet! Having your clothes flapping was much nicer than having them bulging.

Now Marigold had lifted the battered old box off Mark's head. The joke was over, so Penny joined the gang of people crowding round Celeste.

"Can I be first and sign in the silver?"

"Let me be yellow!"

"Bags be green!"

But Celeste hadn't even opened the black book.

"There's nothing to write," she told them. "Everyone had a good time. If someone's unhappy, then it goes in the book. If everyone's happy, then it doesn't."

They all thought about it for a moment. It seemed fair enough, as rules went. Much fairer, anyway, than letting Barry Hunter get away with making people miserable and then saying: "Only a joke. Only a game."

Mark is acting like a robot; turning the incident into fun

teachers notice the changes in the children – they are more positive; they are better able to deal with bullying

this is an important paragraph in summing up Celeste's attitude to bullying

indicates that Mark's reaction is different from usual and what other people expected

Celeste makes a distinction between acts that hurt, which are bullying, and those that people can enjoy, which are not

4: 3: T11: to explore the main issues of a story by writing a story about a dilemma and the main issues it raises for the character

4: 3: T20: to summarise a sentence or paragraph by identifying the most important elements and rewording them in a limited number of words

4: 3: T24: to summarise in writing the key ideas from a paragraph

Journey to Jo'burg

by Beverley Naidoo

Extract 1

Background

This story is set in South Africa in the time of apartheid. Apartheid, among other inequalities, forced black people to live and work only in designated places, identified on the passbooks they had to carry. The apartheid system was eventually abandoned and Nelson Mandela was elected the first black president of South Africa in 1994. In this extract, 13 year old Naledi and her younger brother Tiro have just begun a 300km journey to Johannesburg (Jo'burg) to find their mother who works there as a maid. The children want her to return home, as they are frightened that their baby sister will die.

Shared reading and discussing the text

● The children's understanding of the extract will be improved by some preparatory work explaining the political situation of South African under apartheid and the impact it had on black South Africans' lives.

● Explain that Naledi and Tiro are making the journey because they believed that their mother could save their baby sister's life.

● Read the extract, and ask the class to highlight points in the first half where it states or implies that the children are afraid.

● Can the children identify any clues that suggest Naledi is the elder? Focus their attention on the first two paragraphs and let them discuss them in pairs.

● Discuss Naledi's dilemma. Should she be embarking on this dangerous journey with her younger brother? Spell out the conflict: should she stay or look for her mother? Encourage the children to discuss their views. Then ask the class to form two lines as a 'decision alley'. In role as Naledi, slowly walk down the alley. As you go, the children should offer you advice.

● Focus on the final three paragraphs. Identify how the one beginning *Grown ups were always talking…* gives important information about the pass laws, and the next one explains how the pass laws had affected the family. Point out how this knowledge influences the way the children behave in the *strange town*. Ask the

class to identify the adverbs and adverbial phrases (*So, without even speaking*; *Nervously*) that link sentences together and indicate the children's feelings. Can they find any other evidence of their fear?

● Highlight adverbs and adverbial phrases in the text, for example *quickly, steadily, all too clearly*, and demonstrate how they modify the verbs. Examine how adverbs can be placed in different positions in the sentence, perhaps by using whiteboards or cards to make 'human sentences', with the adverb holder moving about the sentence. Ask whether the change of position alters the meaning.

Activities

● Help the children to identify on a map how far 300km would be from your school. Estimate how long such a walk would take. Use a map of South Africa to mark a radius of 300km from Johannesburg.

● The text will be challenging for less confident readers. Support them in re-reading it, for example by recapping on the significance of the pass laws. Read the song with them.

● Focus on the dilemma facing Naledi. Compose with the children an opening paragraph for a rewrite, discussing the best way to express the issues. Then ask the children to write another paragraph independently, suggesting anything else they think Naledi could have done. Listen to and comment upon different versions. As an independent activity, encourage them to add a final paragraph that explains what they would have done.

● Ask the children to begin a book journal, particularly if they are able to read the rest of the story. At this point, they could be collecting their impressions of the two characters by listing what they know about them so far.

Extension/further reading

The final paragraph could be interpreted effectively through movement. The children should think about the way that actions can convey fear and nervousness.

4: 3: T1: to identify social, moral or cultural issues in stories, e.g. the dilemmas faced by characters and to discuss how the characters deal with them

4: 3: T2: to read stories from other cultures, by focusing on, e.g. differences in place, time, customs, relationships; to identify and discuss recurring themes where appropriate

suggests that Naledi is older, more responsible

they have 300km to walk, and are trying to help save their baby sister, so must keep going

fear seems to be their constant companion

it is dangerous to be a stranger when movement is so tightly controlled

adverbs and adverbial phrases convey the children's fear

Journey to Jo'burg

Extract 1

"Come on! We must get on." Naledi insisted, pulling herself up quickly.

She could tell that Tiro was already tired, but they couldn't afford to stop for long. The sun had already passed its midday position and they didn't seem to have travelled very far.

On they walked, steadily, singing to break the silence.

But in the middle of the afternoon, when the road led into a small town, they stopped singing and began to walk a little faster. They were afraid a policeman might stop them because they were strangers.

Policemen were dangerous. Even in the village they knew that…

The older children at school had made up a song:

"Beware that policeman,
He'll want to see your 'pass'
He'll say its not in order
That day may be your last!"

Grown ups were always talking about this 'pass'. If you wanted to visit some place, the 'pass' must allow it. If you wanted to change your job, the 'pass' must allow it. It seemed everyone in school knew somebody who had been in trouble over the 'pass'.

Naledi and Tiro remembered all too clearly the terrible stories their uncle had told them about a prison farm. One day he had left his 'pass' at home and a policeman had stopped him. That was how he got sent to the prison farm.

So, without even speaking, Naledi and Tiro knew the fear in the other's heart as they walked through the strange town. They longed to look in some of the shop windows, but they did not dare stop. Nervously they hurried along the main street, until they had left the last house of the town behind them.

singing helps to keep their spirits up

they are frightened in the town and they stop singing also to avoid drawing attention to themselves

the pass was a means of controlling and restricting the movement and way of life of black South Africans

breaking pass rules could lead to imprisonment or other punishment

shows the close understanding between the children and that these dangers were a way of life

4: 3: T3: to understand how paragraphs or chapters are used to collect, order and build up ideas

4: 3: T8: to write critically about an issue or dilemma raised in a story, explaining the problem, alternative courses of action and evaluating the writer's solution

4: 3: S4: to understand the use of connectives, e.g. adverbs, adverbial phrases

Journey to Jo'burg

by Beverley Naidoo

Extract 2

Background

The events in this extract occur at the end of Naledi and Tiro's first day of walking. Dineo is their baby sister. This extract gives further insights into apartheid South Africa and the contrast in the lives of blacks and whites. Black children could expect to be treated badly by the majority of the white population.

Shared reading and discussing the text

● Remind the children of their previous reading, recapping on significant elements of the political background. Read the text to get an overall impression of the events described.

● Now re-read the text. Focus on the first paragraph, highlighting how the sight of the orange trees attracted the children. Can the class identify part of the description that seems out of place? (*Barbed wire fences.*) Ask why.

● Ask pairs of children to play the characters, holding a conversation when walking along the fence. You might suggest a first line for the conversation, such as *'Naledi, I'm hungry!'*

● Read the next paragraph. Point out that there is no discussion about whether to take the oranges, Naledi just acts. Identify how the text builds up to the climax of a hand grasping her by focusing on Naledi's climb, the shout, the race for the fence. Notice how economically this is written. Ask what Naledi and Tiro might be thinking at each point.

● Read on to *Naledi pleaded*. Establish how harsh the law is for black people. Discuss whether the children should be considered as thieves. Would the class accept Naledi's excuse?

● Read to the end. Discuss in pairs how our view of the boy changes. (For instance, he tells the children how to eat the oranges without being detected.) Encourage speculation on why our view changes. (He is helping the children now, whereas earlier he seemed to be threatening them.) Remind the children to support ideas with reference to the text.

● Ask the children what they have noticed about the boy who 'guards' the orchard. Little is stated directly, but what can they infer? Let them discuss in pairs questions for which there are no definite answers, such as *Is the boy black or white? Why do you think so?*

Activities

● Ask a group to highlight the words spoken by the characters and use another colour to identify the verbs and adverbs that tell us how the words were said. The children should then read out just the direct speech, using the highlight to help them. Encourage them to experiment with the voice of the boy, to convey the change from *Hey you* to *Don't worry.*

● Most groups would benefit from re-reading the text. With less confident readers, highlight the names and explain complex sentence structures, such as the rapid move in the last paragraph between direct speech and narrative. More able readers would benefit from a discussion of the irony of the last sentence.

● Ask the children to prepare for a debate on the issue of stealing by listing reasons why it might be acceptable and reasons why it is wrong. Then debate the issue, telling children either to argue for one side or another. Link this work to persuasive writing and ask the children to write an argument about the issue.

● Work with a group to compose a brief assessment of the piece, focusing on the topic of stealing. In the first paragraph, encourage the children to identify the issue and how the author introduces it. In the second paragraph, ask the children to write what they think the author's point of view might be, for example that stealing is acceptable when people are starving in a land of plenty. In the third paragraph, they should explain whether they agree with the author's point of view and why.

Extension/further reading

Children could read the rest of the story independently, completing tasks in their book journal. These might include making a map of the route, notes about apartheid and how it made life difficult for the majority of the population, research into Nelson Mandela.

seem out of place in these lovely surroundings; stark image of segregation

oranges are a luxury to these children; much of the orange crop was exported abroad

verbs express the range of movements and the desperate race

makes a link between the boy and the children

Naledi objects to being called a thief; they are hungry and only want a couple of oranges for themselves

emphasises the distance the children still have to go

the boy decides to help them

indicates great size of plantation and vast numbers of fruit

plantation is an attractive place for tired, hungry children

Naledi does not wait to discuss it; her hunger and thirst has already decided for her

climax – by avoiding saying who shouted, the author makes the incident more frightening

surprise – his youth reduces the level of fear, relieves tension

in apartheid South Africa, someone could be shot just for stealing oranges

practical advice

Journey to Jo'burg

Extract 2

On they walked. The sun was low down now and there was a strong smell of oranges coming from rows and rows of orange trees behind barbed wire fences. As far as they could see there were orange trees with dark green leaves and bright round fruit. Oranges were sweet and wonderful to taste and they didn't have them often.

The children looked at each other.

"Do you think we could…" Tiro began.

But Naledi was already carefully pushing apart the barbed wire, edging her body through.

"Keep watch!" she ordered Tiro.

She was on tip-toes, stretching for an orange, when they heard, "HEY YOU!"

Naledi dropped down, then dashed for the fence. Tiro was holding the wires for her. She tried to scramble through, but it was too late. A hand grasped her and pulled her back.

Naledi looked up and saw a young boy, her own age.

"What are you doing?" he demanded.

He spoke in Tswana, their own language.

"The white farmer could kill you if he sees you. Don't you know he has a gun to shoot thieves?"

"We're not thieves. We've been walking all day and we're very hungry. Please don't call him." Naledi pleaded.

The boy looked more friendly now and asked where they came from.

So they told him about Dineo and how they were going to Johannesburg. The boy whistled.

"Phew. So far!"

He paused.

"Look. I know a place where you can sleep tonight and where the farmer won't find you. Stay here and I'll take you there when it's dark."

Naledi and Tiro glanced at each other, still a little nervous.

"Don't worry. You'll be safe waiting here. The farmer has gone inside for his supper," the boy reassured them. Then he grinned. "But if you eat oranges you must hide the peels well or there will be big trouble. We have to pick the fruit, but we're not allowed to eat it."

Lord of the Winds

by Maggie Pearson

Background

This text is from a retelling of a story by James Aggrey, an African writer who died in 1927. *Lord of the Winds* is an allegory, where animals and other characters represent something else, in this case Africa and Europe. When Aggrey was writing, much of Africa was controlled by Europeans. He wanted Africans to remember their past and be as proud and free as eagles.

The extract tells of a hunter who captures an eagle and makes it submit to his will. Some children might be upset by the ill treatment of a wild animal. Deal with this carefully, for example by explaining that the writer is using it as a means of commenting on how groups of people should treat one another. Slavery can also be difficult for children to comprehend, so you will need to discuss this case sensitively and with accuracy.

Shared reading and discussing the text

● Explain the term *allegory*; that sometimes writers use animals to make important points about human behaviour, as in Aesop's fables.
● Remind the children that they have learned something about the mistreatment of black Africans under apartheid from reading extracts from *Journey to Jo'burg*. Explain that *Lord of the Winds* also suggests, in a different way and about a different time, that life for indigenous Africans was difficult under European rule. Explain that here an eagle represents Africa.
● Read and discuss the text. If the eagle is Africa and African people, who does the hunter stand for? Point out why the hunter wants to capture the eagle. Can the children decide what this might mean in human terms? (Some white Europeans wanted to, and thought it was all right to, rule Africa and make its people work for them, sometimes as slaves.)
● Discuss the poetic language of the piece. Short, simple sentences and compound sentences with a strong rhythm are reinforced by powerful verbs and repetition (*It pecked at the hunter's eyes, and the hunter was afraid*) and the fragmentary nature of some lines (*It*

flew down to see) where the movement of the bird is captured. Point out the pattern in lines like *away from the high mountains and through the dark forest… silent trees.*
● Read the next three paragraphs. Ask half the class, in pairs, to consider how the eagle reacted to being in the cage, and the other half how the hunter tried to train it. Then ask the children to swap partners to share their ideas.
● Before re-reading the last paragraph, ask the children to notice the effect that imprisonment has on the eagle.

Activities

● Work with a group to complete the story. In Aggrey's original, the hunter is helped to understand his cruelty and the eagle is released. Talk about how the eagle could be freed (or escape). Having agreed the outline, consider how to link it to the extract. Re-read the final paragraph of the text and compose a bridging paragraph. Then ask the children to write the next part independently.
● Point out the three lines beginning *Mightiest of Hunters*. This is an *apostrophe*, a kind of hymn. It works by identifying synonyms for leader or 'great one' and placing them into contexts appropriate for the eagle. Help the children to continue this 'hymn' to the eagle by looking for other synonyms (for example, prince, chief, warrior) and other contexts (cliffs, clouds, sky). Brainstorm and refine examples so that the lines sound like a hymn of praise.
● Ask groups to research elements of African history, for example the slave trade, the colonisation of Africa in Victorian times, the struggle against apartheid. Ask whether it is fair to suggest that white people treated Africans like the hunter treated the eagle. They could present, for example, five ways in which Africa was like the eagle in the story.

Extension/further reading

The photographs of Ifeoma Onyefulu in *A is for Africa* (Frances Lincoln) can introduce children to African tribes and customs.

4: 3: T1: to identify social, moral or cultural issues in stories; to locate evidence in the text

4: 3: T2: to read stories from other cultures, by focusing on, e.g. differences in place, time, customs, relationships; to identify and discuss recurring themes where appropriate

as it is an allegory, the characters are roles rather than developed individuals

like a hymn, a song of praise (known as an 'apostrophe')

hunter sees how it can exploit the eagle, live off its skills

if the eagle stands for Africa, the hunter is the European settlers

hunter's plan is to imprison the eagle

Lord of the Winds

The hunter walked right through the forest until he came
to the mountains on the other side.
And there, sitting on the highest peak, he saw a golden eagle.
Mightiest of Hunters,
King of the Birds,
Lord of the Winds!
From high in the sky an eagle could see the tiniest movement
of the smallest creature. If only I could catch it, the hunter
thought, I could make it work for me.
Then I could lie in the sun all day and never go short of
food again.

The hunter built a cage of sticks, and left the door open.
The eagle watched him. What was this?
It flew down to see.
It stuck its head inside the cage,
folded its wings,
took one step forward –
then two...
Snap! went the cage door.
The eagle was caught.

The hunter carried the bird home in triumph,
away from the high mountains and through the dark forest.
The eagle's wings beat uselessly against the bars and its cries
re-echoed among the silent trees.

Next day the man set about teaching the eagle to hunt for him.
He wore a thick glove to protect him from its talons.
He tied a leash around its leg, so that it could not fly away.
The eagle spread its wings.
It pecked at the hunter's eyes, and the hunter was afraid.

The hunter threw the pecking eagle into a cage.
"And there you will stay with nothing to eat but bread
and water until you learn to do as I say," he said.

The eagle stayed in its cage for a long time.
Its feathers grew dull, and its eyes shone less brightly.
In the distance, beyond the forest trees, it could see
the mountain tops and the blue, blue sky.

eagle protests against its imprisonment, but it is no use, no one can help it

hunter wants to break the eagle's spirit and bend it to his will

patterned, poetic language

time connective

eagle is still formidable and frightening

imprisonment is worse when you can see freedom and what you have been taken from

effect on the eagle is terrible; realistic; what does it mean in human terms? the contrast with the noble, free, great spirit in the apostrophe highlights the subjugation

4: 3: T15: to produce polished poetry through revision, e.g. deleting words, adding words, changing words, reorganising words and lines, experimenting with figurative language

The Magic Box

by Kit Wright

Background

This is an unusual list-like poem, without a rhyme or sustained rhythm. It has a distinctive layout and pattern and uses language in rich, surprising and lively ways. It uses small details to explore big ideas about what is important and valuable about the world and our lives.

Shared reading and discussing the text

● Read the poem a number of times. Explain that it is an example of free verse. Allow the children the opportunity to explore the poem by reading it aloud to notice the lack of rhyme and the list-like quality. Explore the meanings of some of the lines, but avoid being too definite about interpretation at this stage.

● Discuss the layout of the poem and ask the children to identify the main verses. Explain that they act like paragraphs, collecting and organising ideas, most often under the 'sub-heading' of the refrain. Point out that the poem reads as a list of special objects and feelings.

● Focus on language. Ask the children to find examples of alliteration; adjectives, particularly colour; and opposites, such as *last* and *first*.

● Discuss the individual 'items' the poet will put in his magic box. Many of his suggestions are elusive, but point out how they appeal to the senses, for example they describe or appeal to sights, tastes and sounds. Ask the children to pick out examples. Some of the ideas are apparent contradictions or impossibilities (*black sun, a fifth season*) and jokes (*a cowboy on a broomstick*). Point out how Kit Wright makes everyday things seem extraordinary by juxtaposing unusual ideas (*three violet wishes*).

● Can the children identify how verses 5 and 6 are different from previous ones? (Verse 5 describes what the box is made from, 6 tells what the poet will do with it now it is full.)

Activities

● Let the children work independently to create a 'senses chart' to respond to one of the lines in the poem. The children should write the line out and then divide their paper into five, one section for each sense. Tell them to imagine they are the poet, thinking about *the swish of a silk sari on a summer night*, for instance. What would they see, hear, smell, taste and feel?

● Use the poem as a model for the children's own writing. Discuss what they would put in their own box. Model the use of a repeated line to organise ideas and then write a verse, explaining your word choices. Work collectively to create a new verse. Later the children could write independently, using the agreed first line as a starting point.

● The list form could also be used to structure the children's writing. Parallel themes might include 'In the Attic' or 'The Hidden Cupboard'. Agree a line to link each verse, for example *In the attic I will find…*, and identify different ideas or objects that could be included. You could demonstrate how to write the next three lines, appealing to one of the senses:

A sequined party dress, glistening in the dust,
A cracked old bottle, drowned with
Grandma's scent,
A clock that gave one last tick then fell silent

Then use the opening line again and take other suggestions, following the same pattern. Remind the children how, in Kit Wright's poem, the last two verses move away from the list form. Ask the children to use the last two verses to describe the container or place, and why it is special to them.

● Ask the children to draft ideas about a magic container used to collect special things. In drama, 'remove' different artefacts or memories from the 'box' and ask children to build the story about the artefact by each contributing a few lines. When the story has been developed a little, use techniques like freeze-frame to investigate the possibilities of the story.

Extension/further reading

Gather some anthologies containing poems by Kit Wright. Ask the children to identify a favourite and explain their choice.

4: 3: T4: understand the following terms and identify them in poems: verse, rhyme, rhythm, alliteration

4: 3: T6: to describe how a poet does or does not use rhyme

4: 3: T7: to recognise some simple forms of poetry and their uses

several ways in which the box is magic: it holds such a lot, the things in it are special, some of them are imaginary

alliteration

refrain acts as a way of organising the list of items in the verses

presented as a kind of wish list

opposites

reversal of what's expected

structural change here – 5th verse is about the box itself; 6th is about what he will do in the box, where he will go

The Magic Box

I will put in the box

the swish of a silk sari on a summer night,
fire from the nostrils of a Chinese dragon,
the tip of a tongue touching a tooth.

I will put in the box

a snowman with a rumbling belly,
a sip of the bluest water from Lake Lucerne,
a leaping spark from an electric fish.

I will put in the box

three violet wishes spoken in Gujarati,
the last joke of an ancient uncle
and the first smile of a baby.

I will put in the box

a fifth season and a black sun,
a cowboy on a broomstick
and a witch on a white horse.

My box is fashioned from ice and gold and steel,
with stars on the lid and secrets in the corners.
Its hinges are the toe joints
of dinosaurs.

I shall surf in my box
on the great high-rolling breakers of the wild Atlantic,
then wash ashore on a yellow beach
the colour of the sun.

Kit Wright

images appeal to different senses: touch, hearing, taste and sight

important, moving movements from the beginning and end of life

'impossible' events, but this box is magic

colour adjectives in each verse; some unusual usage – violet wishes?

4: 3: T9: to read further stories or poems by a favourite writer, making comparisons and identifying familiar features of the writer's work

4: 3: T14: to write poems, experimenting with different styles and structures, discuss if and why different forms are more suitable than others

Moon haiku

Background

Originally, haiku were 3-line, 17-syllable poems, with the syllables arranged 5 in the first line, 7 in the second, 5 in the third. In translation from Japanese, this syllabic arrangement is not always easy to achieve. Some of these haiku rhyme the first and third line, which was not done in Japanese. Haiku are a kind of word picture or photograph in words; they are intended to capture a single intense idea or feeling. These share a theme of the moon.

Shared reading and discussing the text

● Explain the background of the haiku form, particularly how it captures a single image or feeling. Read the poems, and ask the children to identify what picture is given by each.

● Explain that a haiku is meant to follow a particular pattern of syllables. Let the children experiment with their names, beating the points of emphasis with their fingers. Return to the poems and ask the class to beat out the syllables. Explain that because English and Japanese are very different languages, a translation that fits the syllabic pattern is difficult. More important is capturing the essence of a scene in very few words.

● Discuss the pictures the poems paint. Explain that haiku convey more than they say directly. They suggest feelings like the sadness in 'In the Moonlight' or raise questions as in 'The Harvest Moon'. Ask the children what 'Full Moon' suggests to them. Is *shadow of the pines* a threatening image of the forest crowding out the house, or is it comforting – trees acting as a protection to the house?

● Ask the children to draw a brief sketch of each haiku, emphasising that they should capture the scene rather than attempt an elaborate illustration. Use these pictures as starting points for discussion. For example, use the image of the shadow in 'Full Moon' to establish the sense of inside and outside; how the light in 'In the Moonlight' gives the scarecrow life and encourages sympathy for him; how by moving his head the poet makes the moon in 'Moon Viewing' appear to hang from a branch; how the harvest moon is so bright that the darkness of night has gone.

● Discuss how the moon appears to have a different character in each poem: powerful enough to bring a scarecrow to life in 'In the Moonlight'; like a huge light bulb or floodlight in 'The Harvest Moon'. What do the children consider it to be like in the other two poems? (Perhaps like a toy in 'Moon Viewing' and a nosy person in 'Full Moon'.)

● Compare the haiku with other poems you have read recently. Apart from subject matter, what other differences are there? Stress that haiku is a very tight form, with no room for 'lazy' words and focused on a single idea.

Activities

● Work with the children to write a haiku. Explain that they must capture the theme as completely as possible. Agree a topic; perhaps a classroom object or the view from the window, and ask the children to list ideas about it. Experiment with a few possibilities before choosing an opening line that sets the scene, for example *Buildings scrape the sky.* In line 2, use a metaphor or simile: *Giant fingers of concrete.* In line 3, introduce a feeling or extend the image: *Ringed with steel. So huge.* Encourage the children to offer suggestions for better word choices, looking to be economical by removing words such as *like*. Rework images to convey a clearer picture or stronger feeling. Check the syllabic pattern, but don't worry if it doesn't fit 5, 7, 5. Draft a title, such as 'Window View', which should sum up the poem.

● Ask the children to work in pairs on another haiku. Take them through the process you had done collectively: agreeing a subject of interest to them; working line by line. Share particular lines and discuss why some work well.

Extension/further reading

Many haiku are included in the *Touchstones* anthologies, edited by Michael and Peter Benton (Hodder & Stoughton).

4: 3: T5: to clap out and count the syllables in each line of regular poetry

4: 3: T6: to describe how a poet does or does not use rhyme

4: 3: T7: to recognise some simple forms of poetry and their uses

haiku do not have rhymes traditionally, but some do in these translations

1st haiku: a still moment at night, noticing that the moon is so bright it shows shadows on the floor; sense of the outside, of nature, coming in

haiku traditionally follow a 5, 7, 5 pattern

Moon haiku

Full Moon
Bright the full moon shines:
on the matting of the floor,
shadow of the pines.

shadow could be comforting or threatening

2nd: more mysterious; moonlight makes the scarecrow almost come to life, and the lonely scene of a man in a field adds to the impact

In the Moonlight
It looks like a man,
the scarecrow in the moonlit night – **8**
and it is pitiful.

8 syllables

scarecrow seems to make poet feel sorry

Moon Viewing
The moon on the pine:
I keep hanging it – taking it off – **9**
and gazing each time.

titles are important; they add to the picture created, sum it up

3rd: poet is moving his/her head thus creating the illusion that the moon is being moved on to the pine to hang like a bauble, then off again

The Harvest Moon
Harvest moon: **3**
around the pond I wander
and the night is gone.

9 syllables

full moon nearest autumn equinox

4th: moon is so bright, and reflecting on water makes twice the light so the poet feels he/she is walking in daylight

3 syllables

4: 3: T14: to write poems, experimenting with different styles and structures, discuss if and why different forms are more suitable than others

4: 3: T15: to produce polished poetry through revision, e.g. deleting words, adding words, changing words, reorganising words and lines, experimenting with figurative language

Timothy Winters by Charles Causley

Background
This is one of a series of poems by Charles Causley. His poems are often deceptively simple, for instance in their use of rhyme and rhythm, and they make you think!

Shared reading and discussing the text
● Explain the content of this poem: a boy who is deprived, who doesn't pay attention at school, and who has a difficult home life, but who, nevertheless, can think about those who are even worse off. The poem is set immediately after World War II, which explains some of the desperate poverty and the language used, such as *Ears like bombs*. Read the poem together.
● Organise the children into groups of three to investigate Timothy's appearance (verses 1 and 2), the way he behaves in school (verse 3) or his home life (verses 4 and 5).
● Having explored their theme, reorganise the class into new groups of three. The easiest way to do this 'jigsaw' is to number children 1 to 3 in their first group and then ask number 1s to make a new group together and so on. They should then share their impressions of Timothy.
● Now re-read the poem. Pause before you read the last two verses. Summarise what Timothy is like, using the groups' ideas. Then introduce the next verses. Explain that they surprise us because Timothy acts in an unexpected way in his concern for others. Discuss the final verse. Does it remind the children of anything? A prayer? Point out the repetition of *Amen* and explain that this traditional ending for a prayer or hymn actually means 'I agree'. Highlight the line in italic – it is as if the poet, like a clergyman, is asking God and the angels to look after Timothy.
● Use the jigsawing technique again to explore the technical elements of the poem: rhythmic pattern, rhyme scheme, figurative language – the similes and metaphors, the use of unusual vocabulary. Share ideas as a whole class.
● Discuss the simple rhyme scheme (rhyming couplets), which gives the poem a light, jaunty feel. This contrasts with the subject matter.

● The images in the poem are vivid and encourage response, so draw out the children's understanding of phrases like *teeth like splinters*. Discuss how similes use *like* or *as* to make a comparison; metaphors compare things more directly. Explain metaphors like *blitz of a boy* and *drinks his cup*. (References to the Welfare State may also need to be explained.)

Activities
● Cut the poem into segments, each of a verse. Can groups reconstruct the poem in a different order, so that it still makes sense? (The final two verses are probably fixed but the first six can, to some extent, be moved around – encourage the children to experiment.) How does their version sound in comparison to the original? Discuss whether their version still gives the sense of Timothy's problems piling up on him.
● Reinforce understanding of the vocabulary and imagery of the poem. Remind the children of helpful strategies for developing their comprehension, for example using a dictionary, making a brief sketch of the object described by a simile. After independent reading, return to the poem to clarify challenging elements.
● Ask a group to create a series of sketches to illustrate the different verses, labelling their pictures using lines or words from the text. Check the accuracy of the pictures on, for example, *his hair is an exclamation mark*.
● Generate an oral reading of the poem. Ask the children to pay particular attention to the 'voice' of the last two verses.
● An intriguing follow-up question for a plenary would be to ask the children whether the poet likes Timothy. There is no right answer, although it is possible to infer in the final verse that he is asking God to look after the boy.

Extension/further reading
Ask the children to make comparisons between this and other poems by Charles Causley, such as 'Figgie Hobbin'. This could be done by asking them to place the poems into an order of preference and explain why.

similes contribute to the overall metaphor: Timothy is like an explosion; violent images sustained throughout the poem and also places it in time: post-war

AABB rhyme scheme

from dirt

hair stands up: uncombed, probably infrequently washed or cut

Timothy Winters

Timothy Winters comes to school A
With eyes as wide as a football pool, A
Ears like bombs and teeth like splinters: B
A blitz of a boy is Timothy Winters. B

His belly is white, his neck is dark,
And his hair is an exclamation mark.
His clothes are enough to scare a crow
And through his britches the blue winds blow.

'trousers'

threadbare trousers let the cold wind turn his legs blue

When teacher talks he won't hear a word
And he shoots down dead the arithmetic-bird,
He licks the patterns off his plate
And he's not even heard of the Welfare State.

does this mean he is disruptive in maths?

which means that he is not receiving help he is entitled to

Timothy Winters has bloody feet
And he lives in a house on Suez Street,
He sleeps in a sack on the kitchen floor
And they say there aren't boys like him any more.

exaggeration shows he doesn't get enough food

if he has shoes, they are too thin to protect his feet

basically says that he lives in real poverty, a problem that society thought it had alleviated

Old Man Winters likes his beer
And his missus ran off with a bombardier,
Grandma sits in the grate with a gin
And Timothy's dosed with an aspirin.

to alleviate hunger pangs?

The Welfare Worker lies awake
But the law's as tricky as a ten-foot snake,
So Timothy Winters drinks his cup
And slowly goes on growing up.

harsh picture of Timothy's home life of neglect and possible abuse

metaphor saying Timothy takes what life gives him

At Morning Prayers the Master helves
For children less fortunate than ourselves,
And the loudest response in the room is when
Timothy Winters roars "Amen!"

'prays'

So come one angel, come on ten:
Timothy Winters says "Amen!
Amen amen amen amen."
Timothy Winters, Lord.
          Amen.

Charles Causley

poet seems to be calling down blessings on Timothy; poem ends like a prayer

great simile! welfare worker worries, but nothing gets done because the law is difficult to grasp and full of loopholes

last 2 verses show that despite his severe hardship, Timothy thinks of others who are worse off than himself

Early in the morning and There once was a man

by Charles Causley

Poems 1 and 2

Background

These two poems illustrate Causley's poetic range. In 'Early in the morning' he writes simply and briefly, but also powerfully about a sunrise. 'There once was a man' is a light-hearted poem with language play and nonsense.

Shared reading and discussing the text

● Read 'Early in the morning' a number of times, clarifying *alarum* as an alarm.

● Look at the first four lines, identifying the rhyme (lines 2 and 4). Ask the children to find the verbs (*hits* and *making*). Point out they are 'ordinary' verbs, not particularly powerful or poetic ones. Ask why a poet might have used such dull language. (To emphasise the everyday nature of the scene.)

● Now look at lines 5 to 8. Identify the continuing rhyme scheme and highlight the verbs. *Fires* and *explodes* convey violence and energy; they are more vivid and interesting than the earlier ones, to convey the effect of the sun blasting the earth with light and colour.

● Examine the figurative language to reinforce understanding of the change from the ordinary to extraordinary. Birds sing *like old alarum clocks* – another homely, everyday image. The sun rises, though, as if fired from a gun.

● Enjoy the poem again before reading 'There once was a man'. Explain that this is a nonsense rhyme about a man called Knocketty Ned. The language is straightforward, although you may want to clarify *brolly, nightcap* and *bonnet*. Ask the children to practise reading verses aloud.

● Highlight the last verse. It is shorter than the others and in italic. Why? (It directly addresses the reader, rather than telling the story.)

● Display the two poems. Can the children find similarities between them, for example the rhyme, the use of everyday language, almost no use of adjectives and adverbs?

● Now discuss the differences. 'Early in the Morning' is focused on a single moment and uses images to convey the effect of the sunrise. 'There once was a man' is narrative, following Knocketty Ned through different events. It is fictitious, whereas the other poem is about a real event.

● Remind the children of 'Timothy Winters' and display it. What can they speculate about Charles Causley from all these poems? Perhaps that he is interested in ordinary things and people, that he has sympathy for people, he likes to tell stories. You could adopt the role of the poet and be interviewed about your work. Ensure that the children check the answers you give against the poems.

Activities

● Ask a group to examine the verbs in 'Early in the morning' by preparing a cloze procedure, with all of the verbs blanked out. Although they can probably remember the originals, can they think of alternative verbs that fit? Make this harder by asking them to find 'everyday' verbs for the first four lines and more powerful verbs for the last four. Discuss their choices.

● 'There once was a man' would, like many of Causley's poems, make a good picture book. Ask the children to sketch how they would illustrate the poem. You might extend this by asking how different children's illustrators, such as Quentin Blake or Anthony Browne, would illustrate Knocketty Ned.

● Encourage groups to develop interpretative readings of the poems. Get them to consider how each poem should be read, using the words like a script, and also how each poem should sound in comparison with the others. Record and improve the attempts.

● Working with a group, invent another character with an alliterative name, for example Skippetty Sue. Think of rhymes, such as *blue* and *flew*, and then write together four lines of a nonsense poem, exploring the possibilities. Ask the children to complete the next four lines and discuss their word choices with them.

Extension/further reading

Ask children to collect other Causley poems. They could list similarities and differences with the poems they have read already.

4: 3: T4: understand the following terms and identify them in poems: verse, ryhme, rhythm

4: 3: T6: to describe how a poet does or does not use rhyme, e.g. every alternate line, rhyming couplets, no rhyme, other patterns of rhyme

simple verbs, almost mundane

simile

old-fashioned language, means 'alarm'

metaphor

very vivid verbs give the sense of the extraordinary nature of something that happens every day

what does the name suggest about him?

alternate rhymes

unusual construction, 'as' here means 'that'

alternate line rhyme scheme

'ordinary' image

dramatic image: although silent, the sun causes a blast of light and colour

nonsense poem; title is like the opening of a limerick; Causley is having fun with language and rhyme

deliberately antiquated terms

italic suggests a different voice is 'speaking'; direct address to reader

Early in the morning

Early in the morning
The water hits the rocks,
The birds are making noises
Like old alarum clocks,
The soldier on the skyline
Fires a golden gun
And over the back of the chimney-stack
Explodes the silent sun.

There once was a man

There was once a man
Called Knocketty Ned
Who wore a cat
On top of his head.
Upstairs, downstairs,
The whole world knew
Wherever he went
The cat went too.

He wore it at work,
He wore it at play
He wore it to town
On market-day
And for fear it should rain
Or the snowflakes fly
He carried a brolly
To keep it dry.

He never did fret
Nor fume because
He always knew
Just where it was.
"And when," said Ned,
"In my bed I lic
there's no better nightcap
Money can buy."

"There's no better bonnet
To be found,"
Said Knocketty Ned,
"The world around.
And furthermore
Was there ever a hat
As scared a mouse
Or scared a rat?"

Did ever you hear
Of a tale like that
As Knocketty Ned's
And the tale of his cat?

Charles Causley

4: 3: T7: to recognise some simple forms of poetry and their uses

4: 3: T9: to read further poems by a favourite writer, making comparisons and identifying familiar features of the writer's work

4: 3: T14: to write poems, experimenting with different styles and structures

Animal Rights and Wrongs
by Lesley Newson

Background

This extract is from the introduction to a book that explores animal welfare. Each section of the book includes factual information, a story that illustrates the issue, and a part entitled *What do you think?*, where readers are prompted to consider the issue. The text uses some generic features of the discussion/persuasive genres, such as an introductory statement, generic pronoun *you* to address the reader, questions to prompt response and make a point.

Shared reading and discussing the text

● Read through the text, highlighting the example scenarios given. Give the children the chance to discuss these in pairs by prompting with questions, such as *What is your view? Do you agree with any of these points?*

● Read the text again. Ask volunteers to underline the imperatives, uses of the pronoun *you* and questions. Explain that in discussion texts, a writer uses these devices to directly address the reader. By writing in this way, arguments are generalised.

● Examine the presentation of the first scenario. Ask the children if it reminds them of anything. Re-read it in order to help them identify the quiz format. Ask why the text might be written in this way. (Quizzes involve readers, you are engaged in the exercise and find that you have become involved in the issue and arguments.)

● Discuss the use of the emotive verb *to beat* in the horseracing example. Ask the children if they can see where it has been used before (in the first sentence.) What does this indicate about the author's point of view about horseracing? Brainstorm a list of other verbs that could have been used and then consider which would fit best and why.

● Explain that many discussion texts begin with a statement of an issue. This extract starts with two examples of the issue. Can the children find where the main issues are introduced? (The last paragraph.) Ask the children to summarise the key points of the paragraph in one sentence.

Activities

● Ask the children to identify similarities and differences in how the two example situations are presented. You could support the inquiry by providing a format, such as a Venn diagram, to collect the information.

● Check the group understands the argument of the text. Then ask them to work out how the first section should be read. If possible, tape the reading so it can be played back for discussion and improvement.

● Demonstrate how to use the quiz-like format in the children's own writing about an animal issue. Explain how to organise alternative ideas in a lettered or numbered list and the use of a stem like *Would you...?* Focusing on another animal issue, such as keeping birds in cages, brainstorm a set of five alternative responses to the issue, and work together to construct a new example.

● Work with a group to construct another situation that illustrates the way that humans use animals. In the horseracing example, this text presents an ordinary activity from a different perspective, the reader encouraged to consider that a jockey using a whip is wrong. Take another very familiar example, perhaps someone taking a dog for a walk. Encourage the group to construct sentences that make this sound a normal activity, then shift the perspective so that it might be interpreted as an example of human mistreatment: *The dog has a lead attached to a collar around its neck and can only walk where the man takes it.* Work through the paragraph together, stopping frequently to check whether the sentences are conveying two sides to the argument.

● Let the children collect illustrations that could accompany this text. Ask them to write captions to link the pictures with the text.

Extension/further reading

Use this extract to draft an opening speech for a debate on the way humans use animals.

Look for materials on both sides of an emotional argument, such as fox hunting.

4: 3: T16: to read, compare and evaluate examples of arguments and discussions, e.g. discussion of issues in books, e.g. animal welfare

4: 3: T17: to notice how arguments are presented

imperative – directly involves reader

stronger verb than 'hitting', for instance

consistent use of this pronoun keeps reader personally involved

ordinary enough scene

emotive language, using the 1st example to influence the reader's response to this one; presents a very different picture from that at the beginning of the paragraph

again, language used to provoke a reaction

straight to the point

quiz-like format gives a number of alternatives for reader to consider

rhetorical questions

it's a good question! it can be inferred that the author sees no significant difference

does this paragraph follow on logically from the examples? perhaps use of animals is not far from abuse or misuse; introduces main issue being discussed; previous paragraphs were giving specific examples of the issue

Animal Rights and Wrongs

Imagine this situation: You look out the window and see a man in the street beating a dog. Would you:

A Go out and try to make the man stop.
B Call the police or your parents.
C Be very upset but too nervous to interfere.
D Do nothing because you think it's none of your business.
E Go out immediately in order to get a better view of the fun.

If you answered A, B, or C, you are a person who believes quite strongly that hurting animals is wrong. If you answered D, you probably don't care much one way or the other. What do you think of a person who gave answer E? Can there be many people who actually enjoy watching an animal being beaten?

Here's another situation: You turn on the television and see a group of men riding horses and making them gallop around a track. After the horses have been running very fast for a minute or so, the men take out their sticks and begin to beat the horses. What would you do: call the police; complain to the television company? Probably not. You might even sit down and watch the race.

Most people believe that beating a dog is cruel but many don't think that horseracing is cruel. Can you think why that might be?

We use animals in many ways. They entertain us, keep us company, feed us, and provide us with living bodies for scientific experiments. There are people who believe that we are often cruel to animals or even that to use animals at all is wrong. They think we should change the way we live in order to make life better for animals.

4: 3: T20: to summarise a paragraph by identifying the most important elements and rewording them in a limited number of words

4: 3: T21: to assemble and sequence points in order to plan the presentation of a point of view

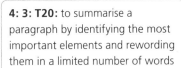 

Why kill whales? by Michael Bright

Background

This text argues that killing whales is wrong. It includes features of a discussion text by recognising that there are different points of view about the subject, but each pro-hunting argument is countered by an anti-hunting statement.

Shared reading and discussing the text

● Show the children the text, explaining that it is about saving whales. Read it together.

● Discuss how certain parts of the text are displayed, such as the quote and more detailed information about something mentioned in the main text.

● Highlight the title, which presents the issue. Can the children predict the subject? (Reasons why whales are killed and, perhaps, reasons why they should not be.)

● Underline the first sentence, identifying the main use of whales today. The next sentence is the key one. Point out how the use of *however* sets up a contrast between now and the past. Re-read the whole paragraph, then talk about reasons why whales were killed. Are some uses better than others? Can the children make a distinction between the use of whales for fashion items (corsets) and using oil for light or food? Encourage more sustained thinking by challenging answers that are simplistic.

● Encourage the class to summarise the point in the first paragraph: that whale products were used for many purposes in the past, most of which have been replaced by inventions, and now whales are killed mainly for meat.

● Look carefully at the second paragraph. Ask the children to find arguments that support hunting. (Japan has a high population but little land available for farming, whaling is just the same as any other kind of fishing.) Can the children find where the writer dismisses this argument? Give them a clue by reminding them that *however* can be used to highlight an alternative point of view.

● Focus on the use of connectives, particularly at the start of sentences. There are some time connectives, for example *now*, but usually they maintain a logical argument or signal alternatives. Underline *Today*; *Over the years*, *however*; *Now* in the first paragraph and *Despite*, *and [it sees]*, *Indeed* and *however* in the second paragraph. Discuss how they signpost the reader through the argument.

Activities

● Work with a group to write a concluding paragraph. Discuss the main point made in each paragraph, then demonstrate how to write the opening sentence of the closing paragraph, signposting the paragraph's subject. Discuss your word choices, and effect(s) you are aiming for. Ask the children to summarise the other arguments in the text and add a concluding sentence that sums up the point of view. Read examples, paying particular attention to how arguments have been pointed to, for example, through use of connectives.

● Ask a group to prepare arguments for a discussion about whales that would support the Japanese embassy's point of view. They should list their points, making notes. Similarly, ask a group to prepare arguments to oppose the Japanese point of view. Structure a debate on the topic and ask the class to decide which arguments were the strongest.

● Encourage children to research the current position on whaling. Set different children different research questions, for example *Are any breeds of whale near extinction? Why is hunting allowed for scientific research?*

● Where it is possible to supplement this unit with information from other sources, you might like the class to write a more extended persuasive piece exploring the arguments for or against whaling. Use shared writing to model the construction of a balanced, but effective persuasive piece.

Extension/further reading

Research the development of whaling and hunting techniques as part of work on the Victorians or Britain since 1930.

this is the real subject, picked up again in paragraph 2

some time connectives

connective introduces an alternative, the writer's, point of view

paragraph 2 presents both sides of the argument, but comes down against eating whale meat

Why kill whales?

Today whales are killed mainly for meat that is eaten in luxury restaurants and homes in Iceland, Norway and Japan. Over the years, however, whales have been killed to provide many products. Blubber used to be boiled down to make oil for oil-lamps or used in the production of margarines and soaps. The sieve-like plates in the mouths of baleen whales were used to stiffen corsets. Vitamin A was obtained from the liver and insulin from the pancreas. Oil from the head of the sperm whale was used to make smokeless candles, for the lubrication of fine machinery and in cosmetics. Now there are substitutes for all whale products. Vegetable oils, for example, are used in margarines and oil from the jojoba bean can replace sperm whale oil.

The Japanese whalers place more importance on whale meat than on oil. Despite a superabundance worldwide of protein-rich foods, such as beef, poultry and dairy products, Japan would like to continue to consume whale meat. Japan is a country with many millions of people squeezed onto a small living space and so there is limited land for agricultural expansion. Japan has a tradition of exploiting the sea as its main food source, and it sees whales as a legitimate part of that harvest. Indeed, the Japanese do not recognise that whaling is cruel. Most whale meat in Japan, however, is not really

Whale oils, particularly those extracted from sperm whales, used to be used in the manufacture of certain expensive lipsticks. Today synthetic oils have replaced whale oils, although in some cosmetics, natural oils from sharks are still used.

supplementing the diet of the Japanese man-in-the-street. It is a luxury food served at the most expensive restaurants.

"Japan cannot accept the argument that whaling is more cruel than the killing of other livestock."

Statement from the Japanese Embassy in London

1st paragraph tells how whale parts were used in the past and why they don't need to be used now

argument that there is no need to kill whales for food as there are more than enough animal products available

perhaps suggests 'taking advantage of'

as demonstrated in the quote

logical connectives when presenting a case

argument that whale meat is not a necessity

The Song of the Whale

by Kit Wright

Background

This poem is an example of persuasive writing, though it is not a traditional persuasive text like an advertisement or letter. It uses almost none of the conventions of persuasive writing, but does argue, powerfully, a strong point of view.

Shared reading and discussing the text

● Ask the children, as they read the poem, to decide what the poet's opinion is about the hunting of whales and be able to back up opinions with evidence from the text. Give them time to re-read, discuss in pairs and report back. Ideally the discussion should identify the poet's outrage that great creatures such as a whale (*heaving mountain in the sea*) are killed for lipstick and shoe polish.

● After the first reading, you may need to clarify the meaning of *kind* and *keening* (mournful crying, wailing) and in what sense faces are *painted*.

● Point out that although there are no rhymes, the poem does have a very strong sense of rhythm. Identify the different forms of punctuation that control the meaning and indicate how the poem should be read.

● Explain that the poet is not hiding his point of view. He highlights our selfishness by stressing the grandeur and sensitivity of the whale.

● Highlight the second verse and the way that the poet describes the whale as *crying*. If possible, play a recording of the creature's distinctive songs. Point out how, in subsequent verses, Kit Wright develops this idea of the cry; it becomes a plaintive call and proud song to and for all whales.

● Ask the class to discuss *How we would use your dying* and the chorus *Lipstick for...* Support the discussion by reading the lines in different tones, for example with a neutral, 'newsreader's voice' and then sadly or angrily. Ask which sounds better. Clarify that the poet is upset at the pointlessness of the whale's death. Highlight the last verse and chorus; the poet seems to suggest that whales will never be safe from man.

Activities

● Explore different interpretations of the poem by asking children to work in pairs to read it aloud. You might suggest a particular mood for the reading, such as angry or sad.

● Discuss with more able readers why this poem is persuasive and makes you think, even though it does not marshal nor generalise arguments. Help them to appreciate how, by focusing on our shameful actions and the whale's qualities, the poet raises our sympathy. This sympathy is itself very persuasive.

● Help a group to compose an additional section for the poem. This would include another verse focusing on the 'whale as a mountain' metaphor and making reference to the whale's song. It should end with the chorus as in the poem.

● Ask the children to research the arguments about whale-hunting and list them in point form. Then work with a group to create a persuasive argument, taking one side. Ensure the piece makes use of persuasive writing features, such as a general opening statement that presents the argument, a series of points to develop ideas, use of examples and illustrations, the present tense and generic terms rather than particular names (*Whales are...*), use of logical connectives (*This shows...*).

● Pick out effective metaphors like *Heaving mountain in the sea* in the poem. Look at some pictures of whales and ask a group to create other images that convey the magnificence of whales by making effective comparisons. You might develop a list poem with them, using Kit Wright's 'The Magic Box' (see page 92) as a model.

Extension/further reading

Children could research information about whales for a poster. This might include parts of the poem and factual information about whales, their habitats, and why they are hunted. They could give their poster a particular bias or purpose, for example to influence children in Japan that hunting whales is wrong.

4: 3: T4: to understand the following terms and identify them in poems: verse, chorus, rhyme, rhythm

4: 3: T6: to describe how a poet does or does not use rhyme

The Song of the Whale

Heaving mountain in the sea,
Whale, I heard you
Grieving.

Great whale, crying for your life,
Crying for your kind, I knew
How we would use
Your dying:

Lipstick for our painted faces,
Polish for our shoes.

Tumbling mountain in the sea,
Whale, I heard you
Calling.

Bird-high notes, keening,
Soaring:
At their edge a tiny drum
Like a heartbeat.

We would make you
Dumb.

In the forest of the sea,
Whale, I heard you
Singing.

Singing to your kind.
We'll never let you be.
Instead of life we choose

Lipstick for our painted faces,
Polish for our shoes.

Kit Wright

title refers to the song the whale 'sings' and this poem as a 'hymn' to the whale

metaphor conveys the sheer size of the whale

deeply emotive – encourages the reader's sympathy and anger

poet contrasts the size and natural presence of the whale with the tiny, insignificant things we use it for

we use products from death for our vanity

repetition emphasises where the whale belongs

addresses the whale directly

punctuation, together with short lines, creates a strong rhythm

the wider 'family' of whales; species

a kind of chorus

another effective metaphor

mournful crying

we, humans, would silence the whale by killing it

links to imagery of whales as mountains

poet reveals his anger here

4: 3: T9: to read further stories or poems by a favourite writer, making comparisons and identifying familiar features of the writer's work

4: 3: T17: to notice how arguments are presented

4: 3: T18: from examples of persuasive writing, to investigate how style and vocabulary are used to convince the intended reader

Jorvik

Background

This text is from a flyer for the Jorvik Viking Museum. Like many flyers, it is a hybrid of persuasive and explanation writing, combining features of advertisement and information. You could link this to history work on the Vikings.

Shared reading and discussing the text

● If some of your class have visited Jorvik, give them an opportunity to talk about it.

● Read the leaflet, then, re-read the main part, which is predominately persuasive. Pick out the imperative verbs, such as *see, Discover* and *get*, which encourage us to visit the centre.

● Highlight the different sizes of font and pictures and ask why these are used. (An eye-catching design makes the leaflet stand out and reflects interesting, lively exhibitions.)

● Draw attention to the use of straplines. Explain that these act rather like sub-headings, which, as well as indicating what is in the paragraph, intend to persuade the reader.

● Focus on the paragraphs beginning *Explore York's history* and *Get 'hands-on'*. Can the children identify the point of view? Explain that the writer is trying to 'sell' the exhibition, to make the reader visit, so is presenting it positively. Ask the children to find the two main arguments made for visiting. (That the exhibition is *authentic* and that it allows visitors to experience what Vikings actually did.) Ask them to decide on one point made in the leaflet that might persuade them to visit.

● Look across the text as a whole. Can the children find some of the different ways that the text says its information is up to date or authentic? Discuss why there is so much repetition. (The exhibition is reinforcing what it sees as its most important selling points.)

● Word choices also present a positive view of the exhibition. Examine, for example, the way some adjectives, such as *authentic, fearsome, fascinating*, heighten a certain impression. (Try reading the sentences without the adjective to make the point.) Collect some of the synonyms for *authentic*, or notice how phrases like *face-

to-face and *hands-on* are then explained in subsequent sentences.

● Explain that one way of identifying a persuasive text is to examine the language. (Persuasive texts are usually written in the present tense, include reference to general rather than specific things and tend to use logical connectives.) Get the children to investigate these features in pairs or small groups. They should notice that part of one paragraph is written in the future and that imperative verbs are repeatedly used. There is an example of time connectives: *Each month*, and other logical connectives, such as *or*.

● Notice that the writing changes towards the end of the leaflet to focus on the practicalities of making a visit. You could illustrate this by asking a series of questions, for example *How long does the museum stay open in February?*

Activities

● Encourage children to clarify the meaning of challenging vocabulary, such as *archaeologists, unearthed, reconstruction, depiction*. They should use a dictionary as well as context and knowledge of similar words.

● Collect some leaflets of local interest and compare them with this example. Establish a set of criteria against which to judge the leaflets, for instance do they use different font sizes, do they include a contact address and telephone number, do they use diagrams? Create a table to allow the children to identify which features are present in each. Discuss, perhaps in a plenary, which of the leaflets is most persuasive: which makes the attraction sound well worth visiting.

● Recap how leaflets and flyers try to make content sound exciting; they are trying to persuasive the reader to do something. Introduce a school event, such as a school fête or a special assembly. Discuss how information could be presented to persuade people to attend. Agree content, then work up an opening paragraph, thinking about a title, heightened language and layout.

4: 3: T18: from examples of persuasive writing, to investigate how style and vocabulary are used to convinve the intended reader

4: 3: T19: to evaluate advertisements for their impact, appeal and honesty, focusing in particular on how information about the product is presented: exaggerated claims, tactics for grabbing attention, linguistic devices, e.g. puns, jingles, alliteration, invented words

flyers often mix persuasive writing with more straightforward information-giving

bulleted list picks out interactive features

use of many imperatives to encourage reader and reflect lively nature of exhibition

reinforce the impression that exhibition presents realistic picture of Viking life

heightened language

JORVIK
THE (AUTHENTIC) VIKING (ENCOUNTER)

Get face-to-face with the Vikings of JORVIK

- see them
- hear them
- smell them
- (talk) to them

(Explore) York's history on the very site where archaeologists unearthed remains of the Viking-Age city of 'JORVIK' in the late 1970s. Discover what life was like here over 1000 years ago, (get) face-to-face with our resident Vikings, and journey through a reconstruction of actual Viking-Age streets, (accurate) to the finest detail.

For details of what's on when visit our website www.vikingjorvik.com or ring 01904 543403.

JORVIK is owned by York Archaeological Trust, a Registered Charity (No. 509060). They uncovered the beautifully preserved remains of Viking-Age Coppergate. The income generated by JORVIK enables the Trust to fund future archaeological activity, including education, excavation, research and the publication of books and papers. By visiting you are helping them to continue this valuable work.

To pre-book your visit ring 01904 543403.

NEW FOR 2003
(FEARSOME) CRAFTSMEN EXHIBITION

Get ('hands-on') in our exciting new exhibition. A fascinating depiction of Viking Age arts and crafts. (Each month) we will focus on a specific craft, with a range of activities and special events: (hear) tales of the warriors' myths and legends in traditional sagas; (witness) duels and battle techniques, or even (dress) as a Viking yourself.

OPENING TIMES 2003/04 April to October (and Jorvik Viking Festival): 10.00–17.00 (last admission) November to March: 10.00–16.00 (last admission) Opening hours over the Christmas and New Year period vary, and we are closed on Christmas Day. Please call 01904 643211 (24-hour automated information) for details.

ADVANCE BOOKINGS Make the most of your time in York by calling our reservations department and pre-booking your visit to JORVIK. Lines are open Monday–Friday 9am–5pm and Saturday 10am–4pm. To take advantage of this service, telephone 01904 543403 with your credit/debit card details and preferred date and time to visit. Please note that this service carries an additional charge at peak periods, and is subject to availability.

JORVIK, Coppergate, York YO1 9WT

use of photographs and different font sizes to emphasise message and make flyer attractive

emphasises interactive nature of exhibition

time connective

active imperative verbs

tone in this section is factual rather than persuasive; information reader needs to know if he or she has been persuaded to visit

4: 3: T25: to design an advertisement, such as a poster on paper or screen, e.g. for a school fête, making use of linguistic and other features learnt from reading examples

4: 3: W15: to use a range of presentational skills, e.g.:
- print script for captions, sub-headings and labels
- capital letters for posters, title pages, headings
- a range of computer generated fonts and point sizes

Charity appeals

Background

These aid 'adverts' were placed in newspapers at Christmas 2002. They refer to the crisis in Africa resulting from drought, political unrest and the slow response from western nations.

Shared reading and discussing the text

● Briefly introduce the texts and read them with the children. Ensure that they understand the main proposition in both: that many people face starvation and disease and need our help.

● Go through one text in detail, noting obvious features, such as the title or strapline, different font sizes and bold print; and less obvious ones like heightened language (*frightening levels, huge, urgently needed, at risk* and so on), the direct appeal for money. Once you have identified a feature, ask the children to mark the same feature in the other text.

● Identify the similarities and differences between the two texts, specifically in terms of the way they present their message. After paired discussion, complete a 'similarities and differences' chart collectively. Similarities include a direct appeal to the reader, a number of points to support their claims; differences include the degree of specificity (the Oxfam appeal talks about *supplying tools and seeds* rather than *emergency programmes*, and the different donation figures suggested).

● Ask the class which of the two appeals is the most persuasive. Ask them to discuss why one works better, in their opinion, than the other. Which appeals more to children and why?

● Notice the ways that the charities try to make donating as easy as possible, for example by giving phone numbers and a coupon. Discuss with the children why it is important to make giving straightforward and of little effort.

● Identify and investigate the connectives in both texts, for example *and, so that, And, But; that, This year, which, along with.* As you would expect, the connectives mainly support the logic of the argument and there are few time connectives; those in the Oxfam piece are simpler than in the Concern one.

Activities

● Help a group to prepare a glossary to explain the specialist terms used in the two adverts.

● Ask groups to complete a chart identifying the features of persuasive texts. You could make this more challenging by requiring examples of the features to be written down.

	Concern	Oxfam
Opening statement that clearly identifies the point being made		
Supporting arguments		
Points in the argument supported by examples		
Summary or reiteration of the opening position		
Present tense		
Focuses on the general not the particular		
Logical rather than time connectives		
Emotive language		

● Ask a group to prepare an advert about the crisis in Africa to appeal to children. Remind them of some of the features of effective adverts, then take them through the process one step at a time. Agree the content of the advert, compose a lead statement, and draft points – each supported by an example. After each stage, stop and discuss children's efforts, encouraging revision as they go along.

● Ask the children to research the promotional and appeals literature of other charities working in Africa, for example Comic Relief, the Red Cross, Action Aid, Christian Aid. Compare these with the Concern and Oxfam appeals and examine them against the criteria for persuasive writing.

Extension/further reading

Use an atlas to trace the extent of the famine across the different African countries. Follow the impact of aid on these countries by collecting newspaper articles about aid projects.

4: 3: T17: to see how arguments are presented, e.g. ordering points to link them together; how statistics can be used to support arguments

4: 3: T18: from examples of persuasive writing, to investigate how style and vocabulary are used to convince the intended reader

both appeals are trying to persuade reader that people in Africa need our aid and that our aid will make a difference

statistics to reinforce point; huge number of people needing help is shocking

urgency

identifies practical things that can be done

series of points about the problem, quite specific

bold print to make the message stand out

direct address to reader; emotional appeal

even the web address includes a message!

main points

acts as a kind of headline – eye-catching

supporting arguments

emotive language emphasises how important reader's help is

practical information to make donating easy

4: 3: T19: to evaluate advertisements for their impact, appeal and honesty, focusing in particular on how information is presented: tactics for grabbing attention, linguistic devices

4: 3: T25: to design an advertisement, making use of linguistic and other features learnt from reading examples

4: 3: S4: to understand the use of connectives, e.g. adverbs, adverbial phrases, conjunctions, to structure an argument

The Outlaw Robin Hood

Robin walked until his anger was cooled by the peace of the forest. Some hours later he was dozing against a tree when the distant sound of vesper bells told him it was time to turn back towards the clearing where the outlaws had their camp.

On his way homewards he came to a swift flowing stream over which a trunk had been laid to serve as a bridge. As Robin stepped onto it, a giant of a man appeared out of the trees on the other bank, and without so much as a glance at Robin he stepped up onto the far end of the trunk.

"Not so fast, good fellow," cried Robin. "I was here before you, and I claim the right to cross first."

"Get out of my way, you dung-beetle," growled the giant, and he lumbered towards Robin so that they met in the middle of the bridge. Robin looked up at his opponent and shivered, for the giant wore a hood, and all that could be seen of his face in the evening shadows was a tangle of beard and a crooked row of teeth.

"It seems like you need a lesson in courtesy," said Robin, and he thumped the giant in the chest. But the giant stood as solid as a rock, and before Robin could strike again he reached out with a huge hand and gave Robin a shove that sent him flying off the bridge into the stream.

Soaked and spluttering, Robin crawled up through the brambles and nettles of the river-bank to find the giant squatting on the ground, with his hands covering his face.

"That was not like me," said the giant. "Not like me at all."

Julian Atterton

The Outlaw Robin Hood

Shaking his head sadly, he looked up at Robin, and after one good look at the giant's face, Robin gave a gasp of recognition.

"I know you," he exclaimed. "You came to my rescue in the market-place of Pontefract when I was fighting for my life against Guy of Gisburn and his men-at-arms."

"Aye, that was me," replied the giant. "I am glad to see you got away alive."

"And ever since I have been wishing we could meet again so I might thank you," said Robin. "Tell me your name."

"John of Melton," said the giant, but he spoke almost as if he were ashamed of the sound of it.

"And I am Robin Hood," said Robin, holding out his hand.

This time it was the giant who gasped. He eyed Robin from head to toe and gave a grim chuckle.

"Robin Hood," he repeated slowly. "That is a name I hear spoken with fear and trembling from Nottingham to Sherburn. And to think I nearly drowned you! I beg your pardon, great outlaw."

"And I will grant it, Little John," said Robin, "but only if tonight you eat supper with myself and my companions."

"Gladly," answered Little John, "for I no longer have a hearth of my own to go to."

"It sounds to me as if there is a tale in that," said Robin. "Perhaps you will tell it as we eat?"

Julian Atterton

Extract 1

The Lady of Fire and Tears

Mother folded her embroidery, placed it in her lap, and folded her hands over it. I lowered my eyes because I couldn't bear to see the hurt in her face. But Meg turned her great sea-green eyes up to look at my mother, pushed her tangled mane of chestnut hair back from her forehead and rested her pointed chin on one hand.

"I was there when they executed Mary Queen of Scots," my mother began. "It was just before I married your father, Will, and before you were born, of course. It was at this time of the year, February. Fifteen eighty-seven, the year before the Great Armada tried to conquer us. I was with Queen Mary in her room when the Earl of Shrewsbury came to her that night – a bitter, mid-winter night like tonight – and told her she would die at dawn, at eight o'clock."

"Where was this?" Meg asked.

"Fortheringhay Castle in Northamptonshire, two hundred miles south of here. A bleak enough place at the best of times, but when you're a prisoner waiting for your execution it is a cold Hell."

"So she knew she was going to die," Meg said.

"Queen Elizabeth had imprisoned her for eighteen years, always threatening to execute her and never having the courage to sign the order. Queen Mary thought she would die a natural death in her prison. She'd already retired to bed that February night. She suffered terribly from rheumatism and needed all my help to rise and get dressed to meet the earl. When he came into her apartment he had the warrant with the yellow wax seal of England on it."

"I couldn't stand that," Meg whispered. "Knowing that you're going to be executed in a few hours' time. It's horrible."

"Queen Mary took the news calmly enough," said my mother. "She asked for a Catholic priest so she could say her final prayers. They refused to allow it, of course."

I shook my head. "It couldn't have done any harm. Not then."

Terry Deary

The Lady of Fire and Tears

"The Queen lay back on the bed and closed her eyes. She couldn't sleep, of course. Not with the marching of the guards outside her door, and the hammering of the carpenters in the great hall. She must have known they were finishing the scaffold that she'd be executed on. She rose at six o'clock and said her prayers alone. At eight she asked me to go with her to the hall. What could I say? I didn't want to see her die, but I couldn't refuse, could I?"

My mother was trembling. Meg touched her hand gently. "No, you couldn't," she murmured.

"We dressed her in her black satin dress. The buttons were black jet trimmed with pearls and made in the shape of acorns. Lovely things. And the sleeves of the dress were slashed to show the purple lining underneath. She had a white veil flowing down her back like a bride. She was a bride going to be married to death."

"Was she afraid?" Meg asked.

"She didn't seem to be. She looked so calm. She petted her little dog and walked down those cold corridors to the great hall."

"They'd have had to carry me," Meg said.

"I didn't know there would be so many people there," my mother said. "Three hundred people crowded into the great hall. The death of a queen is a moment of history. So many people, so quiet. And staring at her. Watching every last movement. Listening to that foolish man, the Dean of Peterborough."

"What did he do?"

"He preached at her and told her to give up her Catholic religion. On and on he went. She simply answered, 'I've lived a Catholic, so I will die a Catholic.'"

"That's what I'd have told him," Meg said fiercely.

Terry Deary

The Terrible Tudors

The Queen's mind was greatly troubled. She signed a death warrant for Mary and gave it to Davison, her secretary. The next day she changed her mind but it was too late. The warrant was delivered and Mary was executed. William Davison was fined heavily and put in the Tower of London.

According to one account, Mary was beheaded by a clumsy executioner who took at least three blows of the axe and a bit of sawing to finish the job. This eyewitness described it…

The executioners desired her to forgive them for her death. She answered, "I forgive you with all my heart for now, I hope, you shall make an end to all my troubles."

Kneeling down upon a cushion, without any fear of death, she spoke a psalm. Then she laid down her head, putting her chin on the block. Lying very still on the block she suffered two strokes with the axe, making very little noise or none at all. And so the executioner cut off her head, sawing one little gristle. He then lifted up her head to the view of all the assembly and cried, "God save the Queen!"

Elizabeth did apologise to Mary's son, James…

My dearest brother, I want you to know the huge grief I feel for something I did not want to happen and that I am innocent in the matter.

So that was all right!

But the Spanish didn't believe in Elizabeth's innocence – they didn't want to. King Philip II of Spain was sick of English ships raiding his own, laden with treasure from his overseas territories. Philip was a Catholic, like Mary. So he used her execution as an excuse to send a huge invasion fleet, the Armada, to take revenge for these English crimes. But that's another story…

Terry Deary and Neil Tonge

Mary Celeste

Only the wind sings
in the riggings,
the hull creaks a lullaby;
a sail lifts gently
like a message
pinned to a vacant sky.
The wheel turns
over bare decks,
shirts flap on a line;
only the song of the lapping waves
beats steady time…

First mate,
off-duty from
the long dawn watch, begins
a letter to his wife, daydreams
of home.

The Captain's wife is late;
the child did not sleep
and breakfast has passed…
She, too, is missing home;
sits down at last to eat,
but can't quite force
the porridge down.
She swallows hard,
slices the top from her egg.

The second mate
is happy.
A four-hour sleep,
full stomach
and a quiet sea
are all he craves.
He has all three.

Shirts washed and hung, beds
made below, decks done, the boy
stitches a torn sail.

The Captain
has a good ear for a tune;
played his child to sleep
on the ship's organ.
Now, music left,
he checks his compass,
lightly tips the wheel,
hopes for a westerly.
Clear sky, a friendly sea,
fair winds for Italy.

The child now sleeps, at last,
head firmly pressed into her pillow
in a deep sea-dream.

Then why are the gulls wheeling
like vultures in the sky?
Why was the child snatched
from her sleep? What drew
the Captain's cry?

Only the wind replies
in the rigging,
and the hull creaks and sighs;
a sail spells out its message
over silent skies.
The wheel still turns
over bare decks,
shirts blow on the line;
the siren-song of lapping waves
still echoes over time.

Judith Nicholls

Legend

I saw three ships go sailing by,
Over the sea, the lifting sea,
And the wind rose in the morning sky,
And one was rigged for a long journey.

The first ship turned towards the west,
Over the sea, the running sea,
And by the wind was all possessed
And carried to a rich country.

The second turned towards the east,
Over the sea, the quaking sea,
And the wind hunted it like a beast
To anchor in captivity.

The third ship drove towards the north,
Over the sea, the darkening sea,
But no breath of wind came forth,
And the decks shone frostily.

The northern sky rose high and black
Over the proud unfruitful sea,
East and west the ships came back
Happily or unhappily:

But the third went wide and far
Into an unforgiving sea
Under a fire-spilling star,
And it was rigged for a long journey.

Philip Larkin

Wind

I pulled a hummingbird out of the sky one day
   but let it go,
I heard a song and carried it with me
   on my cotton streamers,
I dropped it on an ocean and lifted up a wave
   with my bare hands,
I made a whole canefield tremble and bend
   as I ran by,
I pushed a soft cloud from here to there,
I hurried a stream along a pebbled path,
I scooped up a yard of dirt and hurled it in the air,
I lifted a straw hat and sent it flying,
I broke a limb from a guava tree,
I became a breeze, bored and tired,
and hovered and hung and rustled and lay
   where I could.

Dionne Brand

CHARLIE AND THE
CHOCOLATE FACTORY: A PLAY

NARRATOR: I almost forgot… this is our hero – Charlie Bucket. Charlie's a nice boy. Of course he's been starving lately. In fact the whole family has. I'm worried about Charlie, though. Why, did you know that Charlie is so weak from not eating that he walks slowly instead of running like the other kids, so he can save his energy? Well, I've said far too much already. Let's find out what's happening at the Bucket house now… uhh, I'll see you later.

[**NARRATOR** *exits.* **BUCKET FAMILY** *comes to life*]

MR BUCKET: Well, I see that four children have found Golden Tickets. I wonder who the fifth lucky person will be?

GRANDMA JOSEPHINE: I hope it's no one like that repulsive Gloop boy!

GRANDPA GEORGE: Or as spoiled as that Veruca Salt girl!

GRANDMA GEORGINA: Or as beastly as that bubble-popping Violet Beauregarde!

MRS BUCKET: Or living such a useless life as that Teavee boy!

MR BUCKET [*Looking up from his paper*]: It makes you wonder if all children behave like this nowadays… like these brats we've been hearing about.

GRANDPA JOE: Of course not! Some do, of course. In fact, quite a lot of them do. But not all.

MRS BUCKET: And now there's only one ticket left.

GRANDMA JOSEPHINE: Quite so… and just as sure as I'll be having cabbage soup for supper tomorrow, that ticket'll go to some nasty little beast who doesn't deserve it!

GRANDPA JOE: I bet I know somebody who'd like to find a Golden Ticket. How about it, Charlie? You love chocolate more than anyone I ever saw!

CHARLIE: Yes, I sure would, Grandpa Joe! You know… it just about makes me faint when I have to pass Mr Wonka's Chocolate Factory every day as I go to school. The smell of that wonderful chocolate makes me so dreamy that I often fall asleep and bump into Mr Wonka's fence. But I guess I should realize that dreams don't come true. Just imagine! Me imagining that I could win the fifth Golden Ticket. Why, it's… it's… it's pure imagination.

GRANDPA JOE: Well my boy, it may be pure imagination, but I've heard tell that what you imagine sometimes comes true.

CHARLIE: Gee, you really think so, Grandpa Joe? Gee… I wonder…

End of Scene 2

Extract 2

CHARLIE AND THE CHOCOLATE FACTORY: A PLAY

SCENE 3

Bucket home, several days later. **GRANDPARENTS**, **MR** *and* **MRS BUCKET**, *as before.*

MR BUCKET: You know, it sure would have been nice if Charlie had won that fifth Golden Ticket.

MRS BUCKET: You mean with that 10p we gave him for his birthday present yesterday?

MR BUCKET: Yes, the one we gave him to buy the one piece of candy he gets every year.

GRANDMA GEORGINA: And just think how long it took you two to save that 10p.

GRANDPA GEORGE: Yes, now that was really a shame.

GRANDMA JOSEPHINE: But think of how Charlie enjoyed the candy. He just loves Willy Wonka chocolate.

MRS BUCKET: He didn't really *act* that disappointed.

MR BUCKET: No, he didn't —

GRANDPA JOE: Well, he might not have acted disappointed, but that's because he's a fine boy and wouldn't want any of us to feel sorry for him. Why – what boy wouldn't be disappointed? I sure wish he'd won. I'd do anything for that boy. Why I'd even —

CHARLIE [*Running in excitedly*]: Mum! Dad! Grandpa Joe! Grandfolks! You'll never believe it! You'll never believe what happened!

MRS BUCKET: Good gracious, Charlie – what happened?

CHARLIE: Well… I was walking home… and the wind was so cold… and the snow was blowing so hard… and I couldn't see where I was going… and I was looking down to protect my face… and… and —

MR BUCKET [*Excitedly*]: Go on, Charlie… go on, Charlie… what is it?

CHARLIE: And there it was… just lying there in the snow… kind of buried… and I looked around… and no one seemed to look as if they had lost anything… and… and… and so I picked it up and wiped it off… and I couldn't believe my eyes —

Roald Dahl and Richard R George

Hero worship

As Spider-Man fever snares the UK in its web, Buzz! takes a look at the original cartoon superhero and chats to his creator, Stan Lee.

One of this summer's big action blockbusters – the record-breaking new Spider-Man movie – arrives in the UK on June 14, but like most superheroes, the crime-fighting webmaster began life as a humble comic-strip character.

Spider-Man creator Stan Lee grew up during an exciting era when the superheroes of today, such as Superman and Batman, were in their comic book prime. Unlike other superheroes, Stan Lee was keen for his creation to live in the real world as it produced more believable and engaging stories.

"I lived in New York and Marvel Comics was also in New York, so it was easy for me to write the stories if I set them in New York too," Stan explains. "Spider-Man had a real address, he lived in Forrest Hills – and there is a Forrest Hills. He didn't live in Smallville or Gotham City."

Stan had already made his name creating the Fantastic Four, and was eager to continue with his comic book inventions. "After I finished the Fantastic Four, I wanted to create a story with just one hero and I thought, what super-power can I give him?" he recalls. "As you can imagine, the super-power is the key to the whole thing." But what attributes would Stan select to make his new hero a superhero?

"I thought to myself, we already have somebody who is very strong, we have characters that can fly, what can I do?" Stan explains. "I saw a fly crawling up the wall and thought: 'Wouldn't it be cool to have somebody who can crawl up a wall?'… except I probably didn't say: 'Wouldn't it be cool' – because that was so many years ago. I said: 'Wouldn't it be groovy!'"

They all kept on running to raise cash for charities

DOZENS of runners from the Whitby area were among the thousands who took part in the great North Run in Gateshead recently.

Locals of all ages enjoyed the 13.1 mile road race through the streets of Gateshead and Newcastle.

Many were raising money for local good causes or their favourite charities.

And local student Alec Duffield finished in the top ten of the BUPA Junior Great North Fun Run, which a total of 7,000 students took part in on the day before the main run itself.

Here is a look at some of our local competitors and how they fared...

❏ Seventy Eskdale School students (including eight year 10s who transferred from Eskdale to Whitby Community College in September) and thirty parents travelled to Gateshead for the Junior Great North Run. Over 7,000 students participated. Everyone enjoyed the new route which took in the Quayside and the new Millennium Bridge.

Alec Duffield (14) this year came ninth in an amazing time of 1 hour 16 minutes 50 seconds! Mrs Landers (teacher in charge of the library) and Mrs Dixon (the librarian) both ran the course. (Mrs Dixon also ran in Sunday's adult race.)

Esk Valley Coaches (formerly Procters) helped the school by providing coaches at a reduced price, so that all sponsor money collected will go towards purchasing the new microlibrarian system for the school library (whereby students are issued books through a fingerprint recognition system), and Leukaemia Research. The school are hoping to raise approximately £1,500.

Several children from East Whitby Primary School also ran, so there was a real "community feel" to the day.

❏ Siblings Mollie (8) and Charlie (5) Smith raised £200 for Helredale Play Centre funds when they took part in the junior race.

They were delighted to meet ex-boxer and pantomime veteran Frank Bruno and also enjoyed a post-race concert staged by S Club Juniors.

The pair, who live in Whitby, will get to choose what equipment they would like to spend the money on.

Seven feared dead in space shuttle disaster

Staff and agencies
Saturday February 1, 2003

The space shuttle Columbia appears to have broken up in flames over North Texas. It is feared that all seven crew members, six Americans and an Israeli, have been killed.

The American space agency Nasa said that all communications were lost as the shuttle was flying at approximately 12,500 miles per hour, just 16 minutes before it was due to land at the Kennedy space centre. The space agency has not yet confirmed the fate of the shuttle but plans to issue a further public statement shortly.

Local residents in North Texas have reported hearing a 'big bang' similar to a sonic boom and seeing debris falling to the ground, leading to growing fears that the shuttle had broken up on re-entry.

Gary Hunziker in Plano, Texas, said he saw the shuttle flying overhead. "I could see two bright objects flying off each side of it. I just assumed they were chase jets."

"The barn started shaking and we ran out and started looking around," said Benjamin Laster of Kemp, Texas. "I saw a puff of vapour and smoke and saw a big chunk of metal fall."

Nasa warned people on the ground in Texas to stay away from any fallen debris.

President George W. Bush was informed of the situation. Bush administration officials said that they were awaiting updates from Nasa and that they had no immediate information that terrorism was involved. Security had been extraordinarily tight for Columbia's 16-day scientific research mission because of the presence of Ilan Ramon, the first Israeli astronaut.

This was the 113th flight in the shuttle program's 22 years and the 28th flight for Columbia, Nasa's oldest shuttle. It is the second space shuttle disaster in 16 years, following the loss of the Challenger space shuttle in January 1986.

Riding on difficult surfaces

Mountain bikes are designed to cope with extreme conditions, including water, mud, sand, ice and snow. However, you do need to adapt your riding technique in order to stay in control of your bike in these conditions. Below are some tips on how to do this.

Before the crossing

✦ Inspect the stream carefully:

1. How deep is it? If it's higher than your bottom bracket, you'll end up swimming rather than riding through it.

2. Are there many boulders? If so, try to find a smoother part of the stream.

3. Is the current strong? If so, don't risk it.

✦ Lower the seat of your bike. This will make you more stable.

✦ Loosen your toe straps. You may need to remove your feet in a hurry if you lose your balance.

✦ Make sure all the nuts and bolts are done up tightly.

Crossing water

The secret of crossing shallow streams and creeks is to pedal extra hard so you keep going at a fast speed. Your momentum will then carry you over rocks and other obstacles in your way.

1. Approach the stream as quickly as possible. Lean forwards as you enter.

2. Transfer your weight to the back of the bike. This makes it easier for the front wheel to get over rocks and so on.

3. Keep pedalling all the way through if you can. This will help you keep your balance and momentum.

4. Keep your weight over the back wheel as the front wheel climbs out of the stream.

Text © Janet Cook   Image © Raleigh Bikes

Mud, snow, sand and ice

Riding on these treacherous surfaces requires a lot of common sense. In particular, keep away from melting ice, and avoid cycling in deep snow (10cm or 4ins is about the limit). Also, never cycle on these surfaces if there are other vehicles present: they could easily lose control and skid into you.

Make sure you clean your bike thoroughly afterwards.

	Potential Problems	Preparation	Riding tips
Mud and snow	✦Riding fast enough to avoid sinking. ✦Steering. ✦Skidding when climbing. ✦Mud clogging up parts or gear cables freezing.	✦Protect your eyes with fitted glasses. ✦Use knobbly tyres inflated to about 35 psi. ✦Take spray lubricant. It may help free frozen gears.	✦Pedal quickly in a low gear. ✦Break very gently. ✦Steer smoothly. An abrupt turn will cause the front wheel to plough sideways.
Sand	✦Sand on the chain makes it hard to change gear. ✦Sinking. ✦Sand flying in your face.	✦Wear glasses, and wrap a scarf around your face. ✦Don't alter tyre pressure or tread; no tyres grip sand.	✦Stay in a low gear to avoid sinking. ✦Steer very gently. ✦Distribute your weight evenly across the bike.
Ice	✦Skidding. ✦Parts freezing up. ✦Falling off can cause serious injury. Avoid cycling in ice if possible.	✦Use spray lubricant on frozen parts. ✦Neither tyre pressure nor grip make a difference.	✦Go just fast enough to balance. ✦No abrupt moves. ✦If you skid, steer into the skid.

Janet Cook

Robin Hood

According to legend, Robin Hood was an outlaw who lived in Sherwood Forest, Nottinghamshire. He 'stole from the rich and gave to the poor'. Among the 'merry men' who followed him were Little John, Friar Tuck and Will Scarlet. There might have been a real medieval person called Robin Hood, but the legend was probably based on the adventures of several real outlaws, in both Sherwood Forest and Barnsdale Forest, Yorkshire.

The first written record of Robin comes from the 1370s. Travelling minstrels had been spreading his legend for many years before then. By about 1450 Robin Hood plays were being put on. And by 1500 men were dressing up as Robin Hood in May Day games, accompanied by girls dressed as 'Maid Marion', the love of the outlaw's life. Over the centuries descriptions of Robin often changed. But he was always seen as a good Christian, as an enemy of wicked local officials and corrupt clergymen, as a great archer and swordsman, and as a master of disguise. ■

The death of Robin Hood

A legend says that Robin was bled to death by the Prioress of Kirklee Priory, who pretended she was trying to heal him. The story goes that when Robin Hood lay dying, he summoned Little John by blowing his horn three times. When Little John came to him, Robin fired an arrow into the air and asked Little John that he be buried wherever it landed, beneath the greenwood trees.

Oxford University Press

Anansi

Anansi was a trickster-god. He tricked everyone: other gods, human beings, animals, birds and insects. He could take any shape he liked, but he usually went about as a spider. That way, the creatures he was tricking never noticed him, or thought him harmless, until it was too late.

The Asante people of West Africa told the first stories about Anansi, and Africans who were taken as slaves to America and the Caribbean took the stories with them.

One of the best tells how the stories began. Anansi asked Nyankopon the sky-god to sell him a bag of stories, and the sky-god set what he thought was an impossible price: a hornet, a python, a leopard, a ghost and Anansi's own aged mother. But Anansi tricked his mother, a ghost, a leopard, a python and a nest of hornets into an old corn-sack and took them to Nyankopon. As soon as Nyankopon handed over the bag of stories, Anansi took them out one by one, changed the hero's name to Anansi and scattered them on the ground like seeds. However many Anansi stories people tell, hundreds more grow every day.

Stories about tricksters, like Anansi, are common in many countries. The trickster is a joker, a cunning fool and a prankster who does things that seem foolish but often turn out to be wise and clever. ■

Spider stories
Anansi means 'spider' in the Asante language. Among the Asante, it is said, these spider stories are only told at night, perhaps because they have power.
Before the story is told the teller may begin with something like:
"We do not really mean, we do not really mean that what we say is true."
And then the teller will end the story by saying something like:
"This, my spider story, which I have told, if it is sweet, if it is not sweet, take some somewhere else and let some come back to me."

English and Irish tricksters
Robin Goodfellow is the trickster of England. In Ireland he is to be found in the stories of Finn MacCool.

Other tricksters
The Winnebago Sioux, natives of North America, have a trickster called Hare. Brer Rabbit of the deep south of the USA is a trickster of a sort. In New Zealand, the Maoris have Mauii.

See also
Brer Rabbit

A Hole in the Head

Extract 1

And the dog kept barking, barking, barking.

"We've got to do something!" Madi said. "Poor thing, it's tearing its throat to pieces!"

Jonjo stood still and said nothing. He was twelve, old enough to be cautious. Madi was two years younger, young enough to be reckless. She tugged at his arm.

"Please, Jonjo!" she said. "*Please!*"

Jonjo thought, Might as well do what she says. Can't just stand here. Stay still, and your face aches and your fingers stiffen. The cold cuts right into you…

"Come on!" she said, and trotted towards the MetrePak. She couldn't run properly, of course: not in all those layers of auto-heated clothes. He shambled after her. With each step, snow hissed and whispered beneath their boots.

They reached the MetrePak. A curved wedge of snow sealed the lid, but it was not locked. Jonjo pushed his thickly gloved fingers into the recessed handle and pulled. The lid came away. The MetrePak was open.

And there was the dog. Chained to a metal upright. It stopped barking – pulled at its chain, trying to reach them – and stood on its hind legs, scrabbling desperately.

"Good dog," Madi said, moving forward. "Nice dog."

Jonjo held her back. "Careful!" he said.

The dog frantically lunged at them. It twisted its head and gaped its mouth as if it were having a fit. Its collar strangled its throat. Its eyes rolled.

"Good boy," said Jonjo. He kept his voice low and steady. "What's your name, eh? Have you got a name?" Very slowly, he stretched out a hand protected by four thicknesses of fabric.

The dog seemed to have something stuck in its throat. It gasped, mouthed, swung its head. It gaped and showed sharp white teeth. Then, as if it were being sick, it brought up words.

The dog spoke.

"Good dog!" it said. "Good dog good!"

Nicholas Fisk

A Hole in the Head

Extract 2

"Everything's changing so fast. Warming up. The seas getting warmer, swelling up and invading the land."

"Tell me *dramatic* things."

"All right, I'll tell you about the eastern bit of England. The sunken villages, they were dramatic. Wow!"

"Great, tell me."

"They're producing wine all over the southern half. It's got so warm that they've given up growing cereals and taken up wine grapes, bananas and mangoes and all that tropical stuff. Under plastic, of course, but all the same—"

"The *villages.*"

"Oh, all right. You go to the east coast and hire glass-bottomed boats – there's fleets of them for the tourist trade. Great. And we had a boat to ourselves, Mum and I, a lectrilaunch called *Pandora.*"

"Never mind the boat. Could you really see houses under the water?"

"You really could. Streets, roads, fences, the lot. It was weird. I mean, whole lumps of East Anglia are just swamped. They couldn't keep the sea out, the tides got higher and higher and the sea invaded, and all the people had to move inland."

"You could see houses and churches?"

"Everything was just as it was left. You could look down the chimneys of houses, even. See everything: old bikes that had been left behind, the old-style petrol cars they used before Dieselecs came in, even a motor coach. All rusting to nothing. In one place you could still read the signs on the shops."

"I wish I'd been there! It must have been marv!"

Jonjo did not reply at once. Then he said, "It wasn't really. It was sort of sad. But I couldn't stop looking."

"I'd have loved it!"

"I don't think so. After a time, you felt as if… as if you were spying… seeing things you're not supposed to see."

Beyond the Deepwoods

Far far away, jutting out into the emptiness beyond, like the figurehead of a mighty stone ship, is the Edge. A torrent of water pours endlessly over the lip of rock at its overhanging point.

The river here is broad and swollen, and roars as it hurls itself down into the swirling, misty void below. It is difficult to believe that the river – like everything else that is large and loud and full of its own importance – might ever have been any different. Yet the origins of the Edgewater River could scarcely be humbler.

Its source lies far back inland, high up in the dark and forbidding Deepwoods. It is a small, bubbling pool, which spills over as a trickle and down along a bed of sandy gravel, little wider than a piece of rope. Its insignificance is multiplied a thousandfold by the grandeur of the Deepwoods themselves.

Dark and deeply mysterious, the Deepwoods is a harsh and perilous place for those who call it home. And there are many who do. Woodtrolls, slaughterers, gyle goblins, termagant trogs: countless tribes and strange groupings scratch a living in the dappled sunlight and moonglow beneath its lofty canopy.

It is a hard life and one fraught with many dangers – monstrous creatures, flesh-eating trees, marauding hordes of ferocious beasts, both large and small... Yet it can also be profitable, for the succulent fruits and buoyant woods which grow there are highly valued. Sky pirates and merchant Leagues-men vie for trade, and battle it out with one another high up above the endless ocean-green treetops.

Where the clouds descend, there lie the Edgelands, a barren wasteland of swirling mists, spirits and nightmares. Those who lose themselves in the Edgelands face one of two possible fates. The lucky ones will stumble blindly to the cliff edge and plunge to their deaths. The unlucky ones will find themselves in the Twilight Woods.

Paul Stewart

Woof!

Extract 1

There was once a boy who turned into a dog. The boy's name was Eric Banks; he was ten years old. The dog he turned into was a Norfolk terrier.

Eric Banks was a quiet boy, most of the time: 'steady worker', 'methodical', his school reports said. He was the kind of boy who didn't make a rush for the back seat of the bus, or go mad when the first snow fell. He was left-handed, right-footed and rather small for his age. He had freckles.

Eric lived with his parents and his little sister; her name was Emily, she was three. His dad was a postman; his mum had a part-time job in a shop. Eric himself had a paper-round which he shared with his friend, Roy Ackerman. (Actually, he was too young to have the round. It belonged to his cousin. But she had broken her arm, and Eric's dad was a friend of the newsagent… so, Eric was standing in.)

Eric first turned into a dog a little at a time in his own bed. His parents were downstairs watching television. His sister was fast asleep in the next room. The time was ten past nine; the day, Wednesday; the month, June. Until then it had been a normal day for Eric. He'd done his paper-round with Roy, and gone to school. He'd had two helpings of his favourite dinner. He'd played with Emily before tea, and Roy after. He'd watched television, had a shower and gone to bed. Now he was *in* bed and turning into a dog.

It happened like this. Eric was lying on his side with his eyes closed. He was almost asleep. Suddenly, he felt an itch inside the collar of his pyjama jacket. This – although he didn't know it yet – was the fur sprouting.

Woof!

Extract 2

The time it took Eric to turn into a dog – his shape blurring and rippling like a swimmer under water – was about fifteen seconds. The time it took him to become frantic was about five seconds after that. His first action was to begin scrabbling in the bed, trying to get a better look at himself. His thoughts were in turmoil: "I'm a dog! A *dog*!" The next thing he did was try to get out of bed. This wasn't easy for a dog in pyjamas; besides, they were baggy on him now. Eric leapt, and landed in a heap. He kicked his way clear of the trousers and backed out of the jacket. He resisted the urge to growl when one of his claws got caught in a buttonhole. He sat on the floor and thought: "I'm a dog!"

It was now a quarter past nine. The last of the evening sunlight was shining through the green curtains. Everything in the room – furniture and wallpaper, Eric's books and toys, his junior science kit, his clothes laid out on a chair beside the bed – was tinged with green light. Birds were chirruping outside the window. Next door, Mr Phipps was mowing his lawn.

Eric got to his feet – all four of them – and walked uncertainly across the room. He put his front paws on the dressing-table and stared into the mirror. A furry, rather surprised-looking face stared back. "I don't believe it," he thought, and then: "I look like a Norfolk terrier." Eric knew a bit about dogs. He'd done a project on them with Roy in the second year.

Once more Eric sat on the floor. He was bewildered, to say the least. A confusion of questions jostled in his head: "How could it happen? What's the cause of it? Why me?" He went to the window, put his paws on the sill, ducked his head under the curtain and looked out.

Text: Allan Ahlberg   Illustration: Fritz Wegner

STORM

Extract 1

Their cottage stood on its own at the edge of the great marsh, two miles away from the village of Waterslain. That marsh! Empty it looked and silent it seemed, but Annie knew better. She knew about the nests among the flags and rushes, she knew where to find the dark pools teeming with shrimps and scooters. She knew the calls of the seabirds, the sucking sound of draining mud, the wind hissing in the sea lavender.

Everyday in termtime Annie had to walk along this track at the edge of the marsh. She had to take off her shoes and socks to paddle across the ford of the river Rush, the little stream that bumbled all summer, but burbled and bustled all winter when it was sometimes as much as twenty paces across. And then she hurried up the pot-holed lane to the crossroads where the school bus picked her up at twenty to nine and took her into Waterslain.

The only thing that Annie didn't like were the steely winter days when it began to grow dark before she came home from school. The marsh didn't seem such a friendly place then. The wind whined, seabirds screamed. At night, the boggarts and bogles and other marsh spirits showed their horrible faces. Once, Annie had heard the Shuck, the monster dog, coming up behind her and had only just got indoors in time.

Worst of all was the ghost who haunted the ford. Annie's mother said that he didn't mean to harm anyone, he just liked to play tricks on them and scare them. On one occasion Mrs Carter had dropped a basket of shopping into the water, and she complained that the ghost had given her a push from behind. And the farmer, Mr Elkins, told Annie he had heard shouting and whinnying at the ford, but could see no man or horse to go with them. Annie always ran down the lane after school in winter so that she could get past the ford before it was completely dark.

STORM

Extract 2

Annie slipped one hand inside her mother's hand. The hooves drummed louder and louder, almost on top of them, and round the corner of the cottage galloped a horseman on a fine chestnut mare.

"Whoa!" shouted the rider when he saw Annie and her family standing at the cottage door.

"That's not Elkins, then," said Mr Carter, hauling himself in front of his wife and daughters. "That's not his horse."

The horseman stopped just outside the pool of light streaming through the open door, and none of them recognised him. He was tall and unsmiling.

"That's a rough old night," Mr Carter called out.

The horseman nodded and said not a word.

"Are you going into Waterslain?"

"Waterslain?" said the horseman. "Not in particular."

"Blast!" said Mr Carter in a thoughtful kind of way.

"I could go," said the horseman in a dark voice, "if there was a need."

Then Annie's mother loosed her daughter's hand and stepped out into the storm and soon explained the need, and Mr Carter went out and asked the horseman his name. The wind gave a shriek and Annie was unable to catch his reply. "So you see," said Annie's mother, "there's no time to be lost."

"Come on up, Annie," said the horseman.

"It's all right," said Annie, shaking her head.

"I'll take you," said the horseman.

"You'll be fine," said Mrs Carter.

"I can walk," insisted Annie.

But the horseman quickly bent down and put a hand under one of Annie's shoulders and swung her up on to the saddle in front of him as if she were as light as thistledown.

Annie's heart was beating fearfully. She bit hard on her lower lip.

Then the horseman raised one hand and spurred his horse. Mr and Mrs Carter stood and watched as Annie turned away the full white moon of her face and then she and the horseman were swallowed in the stormy darkness.

Kevin Crossley-Holland

Granny Granny Please Comb My Hair

Granny Granny
please comb my hair
you always take your time
you always take such care

You put me to sit on a cushion
between your knees
you rub a little coconut oil
parting gentle as a breeze

Mummy Mummy
She's always in a hurry-hurry
rush
she pulls my hair
sometimes she tugs

But Granny
you have all the time in the world
and when you're finished
you always turn my head and say
"Now who's a nice girl."

Grace Nichols

The Older the Violin the Sweeter the Tune

Me Granny old
Me Granny wise
stories shine like a moon
from inside she eyes.

Me Granny can dance
Me Granny can sing
but she can't play violin.

Yet she always saying,
"Dih older dih violin
de sweeter de tune."

Me Granny must be wiser
than the man inside the moon.

John Agard

Honey I Love

I love
I love a lot of things, a whole lot of things
Like
My cousin comes to visit and you know he's from the South
'Cause every word he says just kind of slides out of his mouth
I like the way he whistles and I like the way he walks
But honey, let me tell you that I LOVE the way he talks
   I love the way my cousin talks
              and

The day is hot and icky and the sun sticks to my skin
Mr Davis turns the hose on, everybody jumps right in
The water stings my stomach and I feel so nice and cool
Honey let me tell you that I LOVE a flying pool
   I love to feel a flying pool
              and

Renee comes out to play and brings her doll without a dress
I make a dress with paper and that doll sure looks a mess
We laugh so loud and long and hard the doll falls to the ground
Honey, let me tell you that I LOVE the laughing sound
   I love to make the laughing sound
              and

My uncle's car is crowded and there's a lot of food to eat
We're going down the country where the church folks like to meet
I'm looking out the window at the cows and trees outside
Honey, let me tell you that I LOVE to take a ride
   I just love to take a family ride
              and

My mama's on the sofa sewing buttons on my coat
I go and sit beside her, I'm through playing with my boat
I hold her arm and kiss it, 'cause it feels so soft and warm
Honey, let me tell you that I LOVE my mama's arm
   I love to kiss my mama's arm
              and

It's not so late at night, but still I'm lying in my bed
I guess I need my rest, at least that's what my mama said
She told me not to cry 'cause she don't want to hear a peep
Honey, let me tell you I DON'T love to go to sleep
   I do not love to go to sleep

But I love
I love a lot of things, a whole lot of things
And honey,
I love you, too.

Eloise Greenfield

Image © Photodisc, Inc

WINDY NIGHTS

Whenever the moon and stars are set,
   Whenever the wind is high,
All night long in the dark and wet,
   A man goes riding by.
Late in the night when the fires are out,
Why does he gallop and gallop about?

Whenever the trees are crying aloud,
   And ships are tossed at sea,
By, on the highway, low and loud,
   By at a gallop goes he.
By at the gallop he goes, and then
By he comes back at the gallop again.

Robert Louis Stevenson

THE LISTENERS

"Is there anybody there?" said the Traveller,
Knocking on the moonlit door;
And his horse in the silence champed the grasses
Of the forest's ferny floor:
And a bird flew up out of the turret,
Above the Traveller's head:
And he smote upon the door again a second time;
"Is there anybody there?" he said.
But no one descended to the Traveller;
No head from the leaf-fringed sill
Leaned over and looked into his grey eyes,
Where he stood perplexed and still.
But only a host of phantom listeners
That dwelt in the lone house then,
Stood listening in the quiet of the moonlight
To that voice from the world of men:
Stood thronging the faint moonbeams on the dark stair,
That goes down to the empty hall,
Harkening in an air stirred and shaken
By the lonely Traveller's call.
And he felt in his heart their strangeness,
Their stillness answering his cry,
While his horse moved, cropping the dark turf,
'Neath the starred and leafy sky;
For he suddenly smote on the door, even
Louder, and lifted his head:–
"Tell them I came, and no one answered,
That I kept my word," he said.
Never the least stir made the listeners,
Though every word he spake
Fell echoing through the shadowiness of the still house
From the one man left awake:
Ay, they heard his foot upon the stirrup,
And the sound of iron on stone,
And how the silence surged softly backward,
When the plunging hoofs were gone.

Walter de la Mare

THE WAY THROUGH THE WOODS

They shut the road through the woods
Seventy years ago.
Weather and rain have undone it again,
And now you would never know
There was once a road through the woods
Before they planted the trees.
It is underneath the coppice and heath,
And the thin anemones.
Only the keeper sees
That, where the ring-dove broods,
And the badgers roll at ease,
There was once a road through the woods.

Yet, if you enter the woods
Of a summer evening late,
When the night-air cools on the trout-ringed pools
Where the otter whistles his mate,
(They fear not men in the woods,
Because they see so few)
You will hear the beat of a horse's feet,
And the swish of a skirt in the dew,
Steadily cantering through
The misty solitudes,
As though they perfectly knew
The old lost road through the woods…
But there is no road through the woods.

Rudyard Kipling

Rivers

What is a river?

A river is formed when water flows naturally between clearly defined banks. The water comes from rain or snow. When rain falls or snow melts, some of the water runs off the land down the steepest slope, forming trickles of water in folds of the land. These trickles eventually merge together to form streams, which join up to form rivers. The streams which join the main river are called tributaries. Some of the rain-water also sinks into the ground, and seeps down through the rocks until it meets a layer of rock which cannot hold any more water. Then the water runs out at the surface to form a spring.

A river gets bigger and bigger as it flows towards the sea, because more and more tributaries join it. The area of land which supplies a river with water is called its drainage basin.

Rivers wear away rocks

Rivers cut into the land and create valleys and gorges. Rushing water has tremendous force. A cubic metre of water weighs a tonne. Water can split rocks just by pounding them. But more important is the load of sediment (stones and sand) the river carries. Rocks and soil are swept along by fast-flowing water, scouring the river bed and banks. Large boulders are bounced along the river bed, scouring out a deeper and deeper channel.

The rate at which the water wears away the land depends partly on how hard the rock is, and partly on the slope of the river. The steeper it is, the greater its power to erode (wear away). Where the land is rising or the sea-level is falling, rivers can cut down through the rocks very fast. The mountains of the Grand Canyon in the United States were rising as the Colorado River cut down through it. Today, the river has cut a gorge 1.5 kilometres (1 mile) deep.

Text © Oxford University Press Image © Corel

Fact File

Longest rivers

The longest river in each continent is:

Africa: Nile 6,670km

S. America: Amazon 6,450km

Asia: Yangtze 6,300km

N. America: Mississippi-Missouri 6,210km

Europe: Volga 3,690 km

Australasia: Murray 3,220km

Most water

Out of all the water that rivers pour into the world's oceans, one fifth comes from the Amazon. It pours out as much in a day as the Thames does in a year. The Amazon pushes back the salt water of the Atlantic for 150km and stains the ocean brown for 300km.

Widest river

The Amazon is so wide that there is an island at its mouth as big as Switzerland. The Amazon is deep, too. Ocean-going ships can travel up the river for 3,200km, right through Brazil to the jungle port of Iquitos in Peru.

Largest delta

The triangular mouth of the Nile reminded ancient geographers of the Greek letter delta (Δ). As a result, a river mouth, where silt has built up, forming a triangular maze of islands and channels, is known as a delta.

The world's largest delta is partly in India and partly in Bangladesh. It is formed by two rivers, the Ganges and the Brahmaputra, and covers an area the size of Scotland. Other famous rivers with deltas include the Mississippi, the Yellow River and the Rhine.

Tidal bores

A rapidly rising ocean flood tide can create a wave that rushes upstream from a river mouth. About 60 of the world's rivers have tidal bores.

The bore of China's Qiantang River can be 7.5 metres high and can travel at 25km per hour. The Amazon's bore is often 4.5 metres high and 16km wide at the river's mouth.

Highest waterfall

The world's highest waterfalls are the Angel Falls, on the Churun River in Venezuela. From top to bottom, they are almost 1km high, 18 times higher than Niagara Falls.

Richard Stephens

Brains

Most animals have a brain that controls thoughts and actions. The brain consists of many nerve cells. Each cell is connected to many other nerve cells, some of which pass information from sense organs, such as ears or eyes, into the brain, while others are connected to nerves that lead from the brain to muscles.

Most of the brain cells in mammals connect to other brain cells and process incoming information, carry out thought processes and make elaborate decisions. Even smaller and less intelligent animals, such as bees, can remember where their hive is and calculate the time of day.

Information from the senses

The sense organs pass information to different parts of the brain as a series of nerve impulses which act as signals. These may be simple signals, giving information about what part of the body has been touched, or a complex series of signals using thousands of nerve cells to let you to see the shape of letters and read the words on this page.

Using information from different parts of the brain, an animal sends signals to its muscles so that it can move in a controlled way. Some movements, such as a single kick, do not require much control, but walking and flying require exact control of the muscles. You would fall over and bump into things if you could not adjust your muscles continually

The brain receives and processes signals from the sense organs to make these adjustments. It connects with nerves in the spinal cord which runs down from the head, inside the backbone. Nerves from the spinal cord connect with muscles, while other nerves from sense cells in the skin and muscles connect back into the spinal cord. Other nerves connect the spinal cord back to the brain.

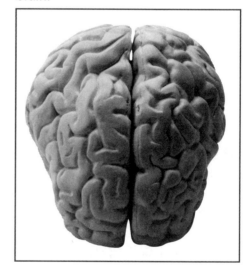

Text © Oxford University Press   Image © Photodisc, Inc

BULGING BRAIN BASICS

What's your brain for?

The brain is the part of your body that tells you what's going on around you. You can use your brain to order your body around and even to order everybody else around. But there's much more to your brain. Much, much more.

Inside your brain are your precious memories, your dreams, your hopes for the future and the knowledge of everything you love and care about. In your brain you can sense lovely smells and tastes and colours. Your brain helps you feel great and happy about life and that's the good side. But your brain also creates horrible fears and worries that can make you miserable.

Your brain makes the thoughts and feelings that make your personality. Your brain turns your body from a living object into *you* the person. Without a brain you'd be as dead as a dodo's tombstone, so it's good to know that you've got your very own bulging brain right now between your ears… hopefully.

Inside the bulging brain

Still want to be a brain surgeon? Excellent. Now you've found out a bit about what the bulging brain does, you're ready to check out how it works…

Bet you never knew!

Your brain weighs less than 1.3 kg — that's a little less than the weight of a large bag of sugar or the weight of all the germs swarming in your guts.

Bulging fact file

NAME: The brain

BASIC FACTS: The brain is made up of three main parts:

FOREBRAIN

HIND-BRAIN

MID-BRAIN

RED STUFF
(SEE BELOW)

SUCK! SUCK!

Each area is made up of smaller bits with different jobs. (For more details see page 32–35.)

DISGUSTING DETAILS: The brain needs energy from the sugar and oxygen carried in the blood. So it sucks in about 750 ml (one pint) of the red stuff every minute. All this hot blood gives out lots of heat – that's why your brain is the hottest part of your body.

Text: Nick Arnold   Illustration: Tony de Saulles

BELLA'S DEN

Extract 1

WE ALWAYS CAME down the lane on our horses. We galloped faster and faster, mud flying round us, with Polly the sheepdog leaping behind. We had to rein the horses in really hard when we got to the farm gate in case they tried to leap over and sent us flying. Then we tethered them to the fence. Bella's was called Lightning and mine was called Splash. We had to leave them at the fence because they'd never make it through the next bit. They weren't really horses, you see. They were bikes.

I'd been playing horses with Bella for weeks before she told me about the next bit. She'd never told anyone else about it, and she had to get to know me pretty well before she told me. I had millions of friends where I lived before, all in my street, and all the way down town to school. But here there was only one person to play with for miles, and that was Bella. And Polly, but you couldn't count on her because she wasn't even allowed out with us at lambing time. So it was a good job I got on with Bella.

I didn't always, though. She had an annoying habit of disappearing. Sometimes, if we had an argument about whose horse had won or whose turn it was to close the farm gate, she would just stand there with her face closing up as if she was thinking, "I don't have to play with you, you know." I'd go back to shut the gate and she'd disappear. I just didn't know how she did it. Polly went too. It was no use waiting for them or shouting their names. I'd just have to wheel my horse back home and sit watching telly, like I used to do when we first came here. She had a secret, Bella had, and she was pretty good at keeping it.

Berlie Doherty

BELLA'S DEN

Extract 2

NEXT DAY I was full of it. "I've seen a fox," I said to my mum. "A real fox. And all its cubs. Three of them! They were playing!"

We were standing in the farmyard as I was telling her this. Bella had just come running towards me from her cottage, and the farmer came out of the lambing shed at the same time. He stood looking down at me.

"Where did you see this fox?" he asked me.

I waved my arm in the direction of Bella's den, and then I saw the look on her face. I couldn't believe what I'd done.

"Where exactly?" he asked.

I shook my head. "I don't remember," I stammered.

Mum looked at me oddly.

"Vixen and three cubs?" the farmer asked me again.

I nodded. I couldn't look him in the eyes any more. I couldn't look at my mum. Bella had turned her back on me. The sandy earth was beginning to swirl around me, and I felt sick at heart.

"You know what foxes do, don't you?" the farmer said. "They bite lambs' heads off!"

Bella started to run back to her cottage. I ran after her. She closed her gate so I couldn't follow her in.

"You're not allowed to go to my den again," she said. Her voice was like ice. "Never, never, never."

I went up to my room, all the joy of last night drained away from me. I wished I could unsay what I'd said. I wished I could say, "It wasn't true. I didn't really see a fox," or "It wasn't over there. It was the other way, over the railway line." But it was too late.

Berlie Doherty

The Angel of Nitshill Road

So Barry Hunter spent more and more of his time mucking about by himself. He was still bullying, but it wasn't the same now that each time he tried it a dozen people came running from far and wide to watch him do his worst, all shouting eagerly:

"Bags be the first witness!"

"No! Let *me*!"

There was still plenty for the Book of Deeds, though. When Celeste opened it on any page, everyone would peer over her shoulder to read it.

Thursday, 4 May

8.46   Barry Hunter wouldn't stop putting his head under Mark's toilet door when he needed to be private. He said it was "only a joke".

Witnesses: Ian. Wayne. Yusef. Mark.

8.56   Barry Hunter kept bumping into people on the way to Assembly. He said "Stop bumping" loudly to everyone he bumped, but it was really him bumping. Paul, Nesa and Zabeen say he wasn't bumping hard, he was just annoying. Wayne says his bump really hurt (and he had to bump back a bit).

Witnesses: Wayne. Zabeen. Nessa. Celeste. Kelly. Ian. Lisa. Penny. Phil. Paul. Mark. Elaine. Yusef. (And Mr Fairway gave Barry one of his looks, so he must have seen too.)

9.50   Barry Hunter sniffed near Marigold and said, "What's that horrible smell?" twice.

9.51   He did it again.

9.53   And again.

Witnesses: Lisa. Penny. Ian. Phil. Nessa. (We didn't ask Marigold because she was upset, and she doesn't sign anyway.)

10.30   Barry Hunter ruined Claire and Elaine's Fashion Show. First he hid some clothes behind the pipes, so there wasn't much time left. Then, when the people in the show were taking their turns to show their fashions off, he started booing loudly. So everyone in the show got embarrassed and wouldn't do it properly. So Mr Fairway stopped the show. (Barry Hunter wasn't the *only* one to boo, but he was *definitely* the one who started it.)

Witnesses: Claire. Elaine. Phil. Ian. Zabeen. Tracey. P.T.O.

Anne Fine

The Angel of Nitshill Road

"Is he *hurt*?"

Like everyone in the playground, Mr Fairway watched Mark swivel his head round as if he were looking for radio signals.

"No," Penny heard him say. "I think he's actually making a bit of a joke of it."

Mrs Brown sounded astonished.

"Mark? Making a joke of something Barry Hunter did to him? Now there's a change!"

Just at that moment, Marigold ran up to offer Mark a guiding hand.

"Am I *dreaming*?" said Mrs Brown. "Is that *Marigold* who just ran up and joined in the game?"

"She was telling them all Bible stories yesterday," said Miss Featherstone.

"I don't believe it!" Mrs Brown said. Then, glancing down, she noticed Penny just beneath the window. Quickly, Penny ran off, pretending she was going to help Marigold steer Mark away from all the people standing around clapping his brilliant robot act. The last thing she overheard was Mrs Brown saying:

"Really, that child Penny's clothes are practically falling off her! It's time she tightened her buttons."

For the twentieth time that day, Penny hitched her skirt up and grinned. She wasn't going to tighten her buttons. Not yet! Having your clothes flapping was much nicer than having them bulging.

Now Marigold had lifted the battered old box off Mark's head. The joke was over, so Penny joined the gang of people crowding round Celeste.

"Can I be first and sign in the silver?"

"Let me be yellow!"

"Bags be green!"

But Celeste hadn't even opened the black book.

"There's nothing to write," she told them. "Everyone had a good time. If someone's unhappy, then it goes in the book. If everyone's happy, then it doesn't."

They all thought about it for a moment. It seemed fair enough, as rules went. Much fairer, anyway, than letting Barry Hunter get away with making people miserable and then saying: "Only a joke. Only a game."

Anne Fine

Journey to Jo'burg

Extract 1

"Come on! We must get on." Naledi insisted, pulling herself up quickly.

She could tell that Tiro was already tired, but they couldn't afford to stop for long. The sun had already passed its midday position and they didn't seem to have travelled very far.

On they walked, steadily, singing to break the silence.

But in the middle of the afternoon, when the road led into a small town, they stopped singing and began to walk a little faster. They were afraid a policeman might stop them because they were strangers.

Policemen were dangerous. Even in the village they knew that…

The older children at school had made up a song:

"Beware that policeman,
He'll want to see your 'pass'
He'll say its not in order
That day may be your last!"

Grown ups were always talking about this 'pass'. If you wanted to visit some place, the 'pass' must allow it. If you wanted to change your job, the 'pass' must allow it. It seemed everyone in school knew somebody who had been in trouble over the 'pass'.

Naledi and Tiro remembered all too clearly the terrible stories their uncle had told them about a prison farm. One day he had left his 'pass' at home and a policeman had stopped him. That was how he got sent to the prison farm.

So, without even speaking, Naledi and Tiro knew the fear in the other's heart as they walked through the strange town. They longed to look in some of the shop windows, but they did not dare stop. Nervously they hurried along the main street, until they had left the last house of the town behind them.

Journey to Jo'burg

Extract 2

On they walked. The sun was low down now and there was a strong smell of oranges coming from rows and rows of orange trees behind barbed wire fences. As far as they could see there were orange trees with dark green leaves and bright round fruit. Oranges were sweet and wonderful to taste and they didn't have them often.

The children looked at each other.

"Do you think we could…" Tiro began.

But Naledi was already carefully pushing apart the barbed wire, edging her body through.

"Keep watch!" she ordered Tiro.

She was on tip-toes, stretching for an orange, when they heard, "HEY YOU!"

Naledi dropped down, then dashed for the fence. Tiro was holding the wires for her. She tried to scramble through, but it was too late. A hand grasped her and pulled her back.

Naledi looked up and saw a young boy, her own age.

"What are you doing?" he demanded.

He spoke in Tswana, their own language.

"The white farmer could kill you if he sees you. Don't you know he has a gun to shoot thieves?"

"We're not thieves. We've been walking all day and we're very hungry. Please don't call him." Naledi pleaded.

The boy looked more friendly now and asked where they came from.

So they told him about Dineo and how they were going to Johannesburg. The boy whistled.

"Phew. So far!"

He paused.

"Look. I know a place where you can sleep tonight and where the farmer won't find you. Stay here and I'll take you there when it's dark."

Naledi and Tiro glanced at each other, still a little nervous.

"Don't worry. You'll be safe waiting here. The farmer has gone inside for his supper," the boy reassured them. Then he grinned. "But if you eat oranges you must hide the peels well or there will be big trouble. We have to pick the fruit, but we're not allowed to eat it."

Beverley Naidoo

Lord of the Winds

The hunter walked right through the forest until he came
to the mountains on the other side.
And there, sitting on the highest peak, he saw a golden eagle.
Mightiest of Hunters,
King of the Birds,
Lord of the Winds!
From high in the sky an eagle could see the tiniest movement
of the smallest creature. If only I could catch it, the hunter
thought, I could make it work for me.
Then I could lie in the sun all day and never go short of
food again.

The hunter built a cage of sticks, and left the door open.
The eagle watched him. What was this?
It flew down to see.
It stuck its head inside the cage,
folded its wings,
took one step forward –
then two…
Snap! went the cage door.
The eagle was caught.

The hunter carried the bird home in triumph,
away from the high mountains and through the dark forest.
The eagle's wings beat uselessly against the bars and its cries
re-echoed among the silent trees.

Next day the man set about teaching the eagle to hunt for him.
He wore a thick glove to protect him from its talons.
He tied a leash around its leg, so that it could not fly away.
The eagle spread its wings.
It pecked at the hunter's eyes, and the hunter was afraid.

The hunter threw the pecking eagle into a cage.
"And there you will stay with nothing to eat but bread
and water until you learn to do as I say," he said.

The eagle stayed in its cage for a long time.
Its feathers grew dull, and its eyes shone less brightly.
In the distance, beyond the forest trees, it could see
the mountain tops and the blue, blue sky.

Maggie Pearson

The Magic Box

I will put in the box

the swish of a silk sari on a summer night,
fire from the nostrils of a Chinese dragon,
the tip of a tongue touching a tooth.

I will put in the box

a snowman with a rumbling belly,
a sip of the bluest water from Lake Lucerne,
a leaping spark from an electric fish.

I will put in the box

three violet wishes spoken in Gujarati,
the last joke of an ancient uncle
and the first smile of a baby.

I will put in the box

a fifth season and a black sun,
a cowboy on a broomstick
and a witch on a white horse.

My box is fashioned from ice and gold and steel,
with stars on the lid and secrets in the corners.
Its hinges are the toe joints
of dinosaurs.

I shall surf in my box
on the great high-rolling breakers of the wild Atlantic,
then wash ashore on a yellow beach
the colour of the sun.

Kit Wright

Moon haiku

Full Moon

Bright the full moon shines:
on the matting of the floor,
shadow of the pines.

In the Moonlight

It looks like a man,
the scarecrow in the moonlit night –
and it is pitiful.

Moon Viewing

The moon on the pine:
I keep hanging it – taking it off –
and gazing each time.

The Harvest Moon

Harvest moon:
around the pond I wander
and the night is gone.

Timothy Winters

Timothy Winters comes to school
With eyes as wide as a football pool,
Ears like bombs and teeth like splinters:
A blitz of a boy is Timothy Winters.

His belly is white, his neck is dark,
And his hair is an exclamation mark.
His clothes are enough to scare a crow
And through his britches the blue winds blow.

When teacher talks he won't hear a word
And he shoots down dead the arithmetic-bird,
He licks the patterns off his plate
And he's not even heard of the Welfare State.

Timothy Winters has bloody feet
And he lives in a house on Suez Street,
He sleeps in a sack on the kitchen floor
And they say there aren't boys like him any more.

Old Man Winters likes his beer
And his missus ran off with a bombardier,
Grandma sits in the grate with a gin
And Timothy's dosed with an aspirin.

The Welfare Worker lies awake
But the law's as tricky as a ten-foot snake,
So Timothy Winters drinks his cup
And slowly goes on growing up.

At Morning Prayers the Master helves
For children less fortunate than ourselves,
And the loudest response in the room is when
Timothy Winters roars "Amen!"

So come one angel, come on ten:
Timothy Winters says "Amen!
Amen amen amen amen."
Timothy Winters, Lord.
                    Amen.

Charles Causley

Early in the morning

Early in the morning
The water hits the rocks,
The birds are making noises
Like old alarum clocks,
The soldier on the skyline
Fires a golden gun
And over the back of the chimney-stack
Explodes the silent sun.

There once was a man

There was once a man
Called Knocketty Ned
Who wore a cat
On top of his head.
Upstairs, downstairs,
The whole world knew
Wherever he went
The cat went too.

He wore it at work,
He wore it at play
He wore it to town
On market-day
And for fear it should rain
Or the snowflakes fly
He carried a brolly
To keep it dry.

He never did fret
Nor fume because
He always knew
Just where it was.
"And when," said Ned,
"In my bed I lie
there's no better nightcap
Money can buy."

"There's no better bonnet
To be found,"
Said Knocketty Ned,
"The world around.
And furthermore
Was there ever a hat
As scared a mouse
Or scared a rat?"

Did ever you hear
Of a tale like that
As Knocketty Ned's
And the tale of his cat?

Charles Causley

Animal Rights and Wrongs

Imagine this situation: You look out the window and see a man in the street beating a dog. Would you:

A   Go out and try to make the man stop.
B   Call the police or your parents.
C   Be very upset but too nervous to interfere.
D   Do nothing because you think it's none of your business.
E   Go out immediately in order to get a better view of the fun.

If you answered A, B, or C, you are a person who believes quite strongly that hurting animals is wrong. If you answered D, you probably don't care much one way or the other. What do you think of a person who gave answer E? Can there be many people who actually enjoy watching an animal being beaten?

Here's another situation: You turn on the television and see a group of men riding horses and making them gallop around a track. After the horses have been running very fast for a minute or so, the men take out their sticks and begin to beat the horses. What would you do: call the police; complain to the television company? Probably not. You might even sit down and watch the race.

Most people believe that beating a dog is cruel but many don't think that horseracing is cruel. Can you think why that might be?

We use animals in many ways. They entertain us, keep us company, feed us, and provide us with living bodies for scientific experiments. There are people who believe that we are often cruel to animals or even that to use animals at all is wrong. They think we should change the way we live in order to make life better for animals.

Text © Lesley Newson   Image © Photodisc, Inc

Why kill whales?

Today whales are killed mainly for meat that is eaten in luxury restaurants and homes in Iceland, Norway and Japan. Over the years, however, whales have been killed to provide many products. Blubber used to be boiled down to make oil for oil-lamps or used in the production of margarines and soaps. The sieve-like plates in the mouths of baleen whales were used to stiffen corsets. Vitamin A was obtained from the liver and insulin from the pancreas. Oil from the head of the sperm whale was used to make smokeless candles, for the lubrication of fine machinery and in cosmetics. Now there are substitutes for all whale products. Vegetable oils, for example, are used in margarines and oil from the jojoba bean can replace sperm whale oil.

The Japanese whalers place more importance on whale meat than on oil. Despite a superabundance worldwide of protein-rich foods, such as beef, poultry and dairy products, Japan would like to continue to consume whale meat. Japan is a country with many millions of people squeezed onto a small living space and so there is limited land for agricultural expansion. Japan has a tradition of exploiting the sea as its main food source, and it sees whales as a legitimate part of that harvest. Indeed, the Japanese do not recognise that whaling is cruel. Most whale meat in Japan, however, is not really supplementing the diet of the Japanese man-in-the street. It is a luxury food served at the most expensive restaurants.

Whale oils, particularly those extracted from sperm whales, used to be used in the manufacture of certain expensive lipsticks. Today synthetic oils have replaced whale oils, although in some cosmetics, natural oils from sharks are still used.

"Japan cannot accept the argument that whaling is more cruel than the killing of other livestock."

Statement from the Japanese Embassy in London

The Song of the Whale

Heaving mountain in the sea,
Whale, I heard you
Grieving.

Great whale, crying for your life,
Crying for your kind, I knew
How we would use
Your dying:

Lipstick for our painted faces,
Polish for our shoes.

Tumbling mountain in the sea,
Whale, I heard you
Calling.

Bird-high notes, keening,
Soaring:
At their edge a tiny drum
Like a heartbeat.

We would make you
Dumb.

In the forest of the sea,
Whale, I heard you
Singing.

Singing to your kind.
We'll never let you be.
Instead of life we choose

Lipstick for our painted faces,
Polish for our shoes.

Kit Wright

JORVIK

THE AUTHENTIC VIKING ENCOUNTER

Get face-to-face with the Vikings of JORVIK

- see them
- hear them
- smell them
- talk to them

Explore York's history on the very site where archaeologists unearthed remains of the Viking-Age city of 'JORVIK' in the late 1970s. Discover what life was like here over 1000 years ago, get face-to-face with our resident Vikings, and journey through a reconstruction of actual Viking-Age streets, accurate to the finest detail.

NEW FOR 2003

FEARSOME CRAFTSMEN EXHIBITION

Get 'hands-on' in our exciting new exhibition. A fascinating depiction of Viking-Age arts and crafts. Each month we will focus on a specific craft, with a range of activities and special events: hear tales of the warriors' myths and legends in traditional sagas; witness duels and battle techniques, or even dress as a Viking yourself.

For details of what's on when visit our website www.vikingjorvik.com or ring 01904 543403.

JORVIK is owned by York Archaeological Trust, a Registered Charity (No. 509060). They uncovered the beautifully preserved remains of Viking-Age Coppergate. The income generated by JORVIK enables the Trust to fund future archaeological activity, including education, excavation, research and the publication of books and papers. By visiting you are helping them to continue this valuable work.

To pre-book your visit ring 01904 543403.

OPENING TIMES 2003/04 April to October (and Jorvik Viking Festival): 10.00–17.00 (last admission)
November to March: 10.00–16.00 (last admission)
Opening hours over the Christmas and New Year period vary, and we are closed on Christmas Day. Please call 01904 643211 (24-hour automated information) for details.

ADVANCE BOOKINGS Make the most of your time in York by calling our reservations department and pre-booking your visit to JORVIK. Lines are open Monday–Friday 9am–5pm and Saturday 10am–4pm. To take advantage of this service, telephone 01904 543403 with your credit/debit card details and preferred date and time to visit. Please note that this service carries an additional charge at peak periods, and is subject to availability.

JORVIK, Coppergate, York YO1 9WT

Charity appeals

FOOD CRISIS

More than 14 million people in Southern Africa need food – now

Crops have failed and without help, millions of ordinary families are struggling to survive. Oxfam is providing food for some of those who are most at risk. We are supplying tools and seeds so that people can irrigate their land and plant new crops. And we will continue to work with people so that they can make a secure living in years to come. But, with your help, we can do more.

£25 could feed a family for one month. Your money will help to save lives.

☎ **0845 300 7070**

or donate online: **www.oxfam.org.uk/dontforgetafrica**

or send your gift with the coupon below to Oxfam Southern Africa Food Crisis Appeal, Room BBg204, FREEPOST (SCE13850), Oxford OX2 7BR

▌ **Yes, I want to help. Here is my gift of:**

▌ £25 ☐ £50 ☐ £100 ☐ £1,000 ☐   other £ _____

▌ I enclose a cheque/postal order (made payable to Oxfam)

Title   First name   Surname _____

Address _____

_____ Postcode _____

Please send to: Oxfam Southern Africa Food Crisis Appeal, Room BBG204, FREEPOST (SCE 13850), Oxford OX2 7BR

giftaid it

☐ Please tick here if you want Oxfam to reclaim the tax on this and any future donations you make. You must have paid income or capital gains tax in the UK equal to the tax that will be reclaimed by Oxfam (currently 28p for each £1 you give).

☐ Tick here if you don't want your details to be shared with like-minded organisations

Oxfam

Oxfam GB is a member of Oxfam International. Registered charity no 202918

Frightening levels of malnutrition found in Ethiopia and Eritrea

Photograph: Pieternella Pieterse
Toyba Hussein has his arm measured at a Concern Centre, Gelsa, Wollo, Ethiopia

Ethiopia is facing a food crisis that could be far bigger than the 1984 famine that killed nearly one million people.

Years of poor rainfall and soil erosion have left millions of people living on the edge of survival. This year, the rains which farmers depend on for food have failed all over Ethiopia and Eritrea.

The scale of the crisis, which comes on the top of the existing food emergency in Southern Africa is huge. 2 million tonnes of grain is urgently needed along with specialist food and medicine for children. Concern has launched emergency programmes in the Wollo and Weylitta regions of Ethiopia and in Eritrea.

- **£50** could help feed a hungry family.
- **£100** could help set up a feeding centre that will provide life-saving food supplements and medicine for hundreds of children.

Recognised as a charity in Northern Ireland by the Inland Revenue Ref No. XN74435 www.concern.net

Call ☎ **0800 410 510** or cut the coupon to give life saving aid.

I will help save lives by giving £ _____ ✂

(Please make your cheque payable to Concern)

OR debit my Visa/Amex/Switch/CAF card:

Card No. _____

Expiry Date __ / __   Switch only Issue No. ☐   Start Date __ / __

Signature _____   Today's Date __ / __ / __

Title   First Name   Surname _____

Address _____

_____

Postcode _____   Email _____

Tel No. _____   Mobile No. _____

Call 0800 410 510 now OR return the coupon to:
Concern, FREEPOST BEL1098/1, London SW11 1BR.
www.concern.net   ERAD03-01/007

A company limited by guarantee, registered in England and Scotland and incorporated in Northern Ireland. Recognised as a charity in Northern Ireland by the Inland Revenue Ref No. XN74435

CONCERN WE'RE IN THIS TOGETHER

Acknowledgements

The publishers gratefully acknowledge permission to reproduce the following copyright material:

A&C Black Publishers Limited for an extract from *Animal Rights and Wrongs* by Lesley Newson © 1989, Lesley Newson (1989, A&C Black). **Dionne Brand** for 'Wind' from *Earth Magic* by Dionne Brand © Dionne Brand (Sister Vision Press, Toronto). **Concern Worldwide** for the use of a press advertisement © Concern Worldwide, www.concern.net **Curtis Brown Limited, London** on behalf of Grace Nichols for 'Granny Granny Please Comb My Hair' by Grace Nichols from *Can I Buy A Slice of Sky?* edited by Grace Nichols © 1991, Grace Nichols (1991, Blackie & Son). **Egmont Books Limited** for extracts from *Storm* by Kevin Crossley-Holland © 1985, Kevin Crossley-Holland (1985, Mammoth); for extracts from *The Angel of Nitshill Road* by Anne Fine © 1992, Anne Fine (1992, Egmont Books); for use of an extract from *Bella's Den* by Berlie Doherty © 1995, Berlie Doherty (1995, Mammoth). **Faber & Faber** for an extract from 'Legend' from *The North Ship* appears in *Collected Poems* by Philip Larkin © Philip Larkin (Faber and Faber). **Guardian Newspapers Ltd** for 'Seven feared dead in space shuttle disaster' from the Guardian Unlimited website 1 February 2003 © 2003, Guardian (2003, www.guardian.co.uk) **David Higham Associates** for extracts from *Charlie and the Chocolate Factory: A Play* by Roald Dahl and Richard R George © 1976, Roald Dahl and Richard R George (1976, Alfred A Knopf Inc, New York); for use of 'Timothy Winters' from *Going to the Fair* by Charles Causley © 1994, Charles Causley (1994, Viking Kestrel); for use of 'There once was a man' from *All Day Saturday and Other Poems* by Charles Causley © 1994, Charles Causley (Macmillan Children's Books) and 'Early in the morning' from *Selected Poems for Children* by Charles Causley © 1997, Charles Causley (1997, Macmillan Children's Books). **Jorvik Centre** for an extract and photographs from the 2003 Jorvik leaflet © 2003, Jorvik (2003, Jorvik). **Magi Publications** for an extract from *Lord of the Winds* by Maggie Pearson © 1996, Maggie Pearson (1996, Magi Publications). **News International Syndication** for an extract from the article 'Buzz – Spiderman Hero Worship' by David Coombs from 'Funday Times', London in the *Sunday Times*, 26 May 2002 © 2002, The Sunday Times Limited, London. **Judith Nicholls** for 'Mary Celeste' from *Midnight Forest* by Judith Nicholls © 1987, Judith Nicholls (1987, Faber & Faber). **Orion Children's Books** for extracts from *The Lady of Fire and Tears* by Terry Deary © 1998, Terry Deary (1998, Orion Children's Books). **Oxfam UK** for the advertisement 'Food Crisis' © 2002, Oxfam (Oxfam, 274 Banbury Road, Oxford, OX2 7DZ). **Oxford University Press** for extracts 'Robin Hood', 'Anansi', 'Rivers' and 'Brains' from *Oxford Children's Encyclopedia* © 1996, Oxford University Press (1996, Oxford University Press). **Pearson Education** for extracts from *Journey to Jo'burg* by Beverley Naidoo © 1987, Beverley Naidoo (1987, Armada). **The Penguin Group UK** for an extract and illustrations from *Woof!* by Allan Ahlberg text © 1986, Allan Ahlberg, illustrations © 1986, Fritz Wegner (1986, Viking Kestrel). **The Random House Group** for an extract from *Beyond the Deepwoods* by Paul Stewart © 1998, Paul Stewart (1998, Doubleday). **Raleigh Ltd** for a photograph of children with bikes © 2002 Raleigh. **Scholastic Children's Books** for an extract from *Bulging Brains* by Nick Arnold text © 1999, Nick Arnold © illustrations 1999, Tony de Saulles (1999, Hippo); for an extract from *The Terrible Tudors* by Terry Deary and Neil Tonge © 1993, Terry Deary and Neil Tonge (1993, Hippo). **Caroline Sheldon Literary Agency** for 'The Older the Violin the Sweeter the Tune' by John Agard from *Say It Again, Granny* edited by Grace Nichols © 1986, John Agard (1986, Bodley Head). **The Society of Authors** as the representatives of Literary Trustees of Walter de la Mare for 'The Listeners' from *The Complete Poems of Walter de la Mare* © 1969, Walter de la Mare (1969, Faber & Faber). **Usborne Publishing** for extracts from *Usborne Superskills – Mountain Bikes* by Janet Cook © 1990, Usborne Publishing (1990, Usborne Publishing). **Walker Books Limited** for extracts from *The Outlaw Robin Hood* by Julian Atterton © 1987, Julian Atterton (1987, Walker Books Ltd); for extracts from *A Hole in the Head* by Nicholas Fisk © 1991, Nicholas Fisk (1991, Walker Books Ltd). **A P Watt Ltd** on behalf of The National Trust for Places of Historical Interest or Natural Beauty for 'The Way Through the Woods' from *Selected Poetry* by Rudyard Kipling edited by Craig Raine © Rudyard Kipling (1992, Penguin). **The Watts Group** for an extract from *Saving the Whale* by Michael Bright © 1987, Michael Bright (1987, Aladdin Books). **Kit Wright** for 'The Magic Box' from *Cat Among the Pigeons* by Kit Wright © 1987, Kit Wright (1987, Viking Kestrel); for 'The Song of the Whale' from *Hot Dog and Other Poems* by Kit Wright © 1981, Kit Wright (1981, Viking Kestrel). **Yorkshire Regional Newspapers** for an extract from 'They all kept on running to raise cash for charities' from the *Whitby Gazette*, 15 October 2002 © Yorkshire Regional Newspapers.

Every effort has been made to trace copyright holders for the works reproduced in this book, and the publishers apologise for any inadvertent omissions.